I

---

The prose and poetry presented herein are products of the Writers' Workshop of the San Diego Community College District, Continuing Education Program, under the nurturing guidance of Donna Boyle.

The authors have selected their best works to engage, surprise and amuse you. Some like fruits will nourish, others like fig leaves will keep things hidden, waiting for your discovery. A few will grab you and won't let go.

The craft of writing is hard work, the reading pleasurable. Give some thought to the prose and take a minute to re-read the poetry. You'll be glad you did.

We want to remember John Orcutt, fellow-author, friend, and WWII veteran. John gave us immense pleasure with his writings and his wonderful sense of humor. We miss you, John.

# Acknowledgments

This book was made possible by the many writers who put their work on display, laboring alongside the Editorial Committee to craft each piece into the finest prose or poetry they could write. We appreciate their courage and generosity.

We wish to thank Donna Boyle for bringing her knowledge, love of writing, and witty wisdom to each class session. She teaches the art of better writing without endangering anyone's enthusiasm and keeps the classroom atmosphere positive and stimulating.

We want to express our gratitude to the San Diego Community College District and its Continuing Education College of the Emeriti for offering these Writers' Workshops.

The Point Loma Assembly Clubhouse provides us in a spacious and comfortable room. Here, workshop participants present their original compositions to a welcoming circle of writers and receive positive, helpful critiques along with ideas to ponder.

The Editorial Committee
> Chris Britton
> Tim Calaway
> Richard Gilbert
> Bill Houlihan
> Susie Parker
> Frank Primiano
> Erika Toraya

# Fruits
# &
# Fig Leaves

## Prose & Poetry from
## a Writers' Workshop

# FRUITS & FIG LEAVES
Prose & Poetry from a Writers' Workshop

ISBN-13: 978-1500698584
ISBN-10: 150069858X

Authors: Various

Printed as works of fiction and non-fiction in the U.S.A.

Cover Design by Tim Shortt

Interior Design and layout by David S. Larson

# Contents

Rules and Regulations *by Rita Early* — 1

Dear Alexander Hamilton *by Robert McLoughlin* — 3

Cowboy State of Mind *by Christopher Britton* — 4

No – No – No Abby *by Shelly Burdette-Taylor* — 12

Living at Walmart *by Mary Carnes* — 13

Smile, Sarah *by Jeff Curtiss Welch* — 16

Utopia Ubetcha *by Robert McLoughlin* — 21

Hi Tech, Bye Simple *by Erika Toraya* — 22

The Wave *by Dave Schmidt* — 24

Just Flowers *by Jeff Curtiss Welch* — 25

Why Write? Why I Write *by Robert Ross* — 28

Searching for Security *by Nancy Foley* — 32

Sweet Memories *by Jene Alan* — 36

Does She Feel Me? *by Wallace Watson* — 37

Winter Flight North *by Jean E. Taddonio* — 38

Follow Your Gut *by Rita Early* — 39

Masquerade *by Nancy Foley* — 41

Vanity *by Linda Smith* — 42

Silly Words *by Tim Calaway* — 44

Ruins are Alive *by Erika Toraya* — 45

Night *by Rebecca Johnson* — 48

Ode to the Microbe *by Susie Parker* — 49

Moment of Joy *by Nui Rehfuss* — 50

If Only You Could See *by Nancy Foley* — 52

Our American *by Tim Calaway* — 54

What to Do About Julie *by Donna Ferguson* — 55

First Snow *by Harry Field* — 66

# Contents

Grandma Nancy *by Joe Torricelli*     67

Minstrel Man *by Cheri LaLone*     68

Reflections on Cuba *by Robert Ross*     69

Golda, May You Someday Rest in Peace *by Morris Crisci*     75

Silence *by Rebecca Johnson*     81

Hibou The Owl *by Robert McLoughlin*     82

F243 *by K. J. Baird*     83

John F. Kennedy ... shot *by Norma Kipp Avendano*     86

Journey-of-Life *by Nui Rehfuss*     89

Haircut *by Rita Early*     91

The Replacement *by Frank Primiano*     92

Compost *by Jean E. Taddonio*     99

Under New Management *by Alastair McAulay*     100

A good intention clothes itself in sudden power
     *by Lindsay Elise Reph*     103

One Simple Stitch *by Lindsay Elise Reph*     106

Damocles' Sword *by Lloyd Hill*     109

Crows *by Tim Calaway*     110

A Midsummer Night's Dream *by Robert McLoughlin*     111

Dream Driver *by Lloyd Hill*     112

Sky Dare *by Jean E. Taddonio*     114

Snuffy *by David S. Larson*     120

The Comics *by Mary Carnes*     122

Uninvited Guests *by Bil Fuhrer*     125

Broken Mirror *by Lloyd Hill*     129

Night Life *by Lloyd Hill*     131

Alma Street *by Linda Smith*     133

# Contents

A Day On The Beach *by Rebecca Johnson*      138

Senses *by Tim Calaway*      140

Recipe *by Linda Smith*      141

Freedom from FEAR *by Dave Schmidt*      143

The Circle of Life *by Mary Carnes*      145

Post Manumission *by Joe Torricelli*      148

Another Sunset *by Paul Ford*      149

Before I Sleep *by Wallace Watson*      155

Changeling *by Harry Field*      156

Summer Camp 1974 *by Linda Smith*      158

Enchantress *by Tim Calaway*      163

Maggie *by Erika Toraya*      164

Nothing for It *by Avery Kerr*      167

My World from A to Z *by Marion Kahn*      173

Restless Woman *by Jean E. Taddonio*      174

On This Day *by Nancy Foley*      175

A Day at Mercy General *by Rebecca Johnson*      176

D' Light *by Wallace Watson*      179

Meeting Pete Seeger *by Marion Kahn*      181

Sunset Mood *by Georgeanna Holmes*      182

Fruits and Fig Leaves *by Georgeanna Holmes*      183

Two Songs *by Norma Kipp Avendano*      184

Don't Do It To Yourself *by Joe Torricelli*      191

Tee-Hee-Hee *by Shelly Burdette-Taylor*      192

When Love Doesn't Heal *by Katherine A. Porter*      193

Intelligent Life *by Bil Fuhrer*      194

Virginity *by Cheri LaLone*      196

# Contents

I Always Knew I Could Fly *by Jene Alan* 198

The Talk *by Christopher Britton* 199

A Real Girl *by Jene Alan* 205

Darkness *by Dave Schmidt* 206

Mother Rose *by Elaine M. Fuller-Zachey* 207

God's Gardener *by Elaine M. Fuller-Zachey* 208

Transcended *by Elaine M. Fuller-Zachey* 212

For the Bride, Ora Lee *by Elaine M. Fuller-Zachey* 213

Sorry *by Rita Early* 214

Walking the Dog *by Shelly Burdette-Taylor* 215

The Third Time I Performed CPR *by Helen Antoniak* 216

My Daughter *by Jeff Curtiss Welch* 220

From Dreams *by Dave Schmidt* 221

Quarantine Creativity *by Nancy Foley* 222

What's in a Name *by Marion Kahn* 226

Go For It *by Jene Alan* 229

La Matinana *by Joe Torricelli* 231

In Motion *by Dave Schmidt* 232

The DMV *by Joe Torricelli* 233

Why I Write Poetry *by Lloyd Hill* 234

Where Do Babies Come From *by Cheri LaLone* 236

Paradise Ridge Vineyards *by Michele Garb* 239

Take Me *by Avery Kerr* 241

Fear of Wind *by Nita Blair* 246

In Celebration of Your Life *by Norma Kipp Avendano* 251

Lessons from the Wave *by Erika Toraya* 254

James Frederick Parker, Jr. 1945-1969 *by Susie Parker* 257

# Contents

Again *by David S. Larson* — 262

We Stand *by Erika Toraya* — 266

Be My Valentine *by Rita Early* — 269

Honoring Adonis *by Shelly Burdette-Taylor* — 271

Mixed Up *by Rebecca Johnson* — 272

Cut Me Some Slack *by Jim Crakes* — 273

Do You Remember? *by Robert McLoughlin* — 274

Choices *by Frank Primiano* — 277

Author Biographies — 282

# Rules and Regulations

*By Rita Early*

WE all have our own horror stories when it comes to airline travel: lost luggage, delayed or canceled flights. But as of late I've noticed that we passengers create just as many headaches as the airlines. For example, the standard piece of carry-on luggage allowed in the overhead compartment has specific lengths and widths. It may not be common knowledge what those exact dimensions are, but there are charts to help you get the general idea – small.

Many of the flight attendants are patient and stand by watching weary travelers shove and cram their luggage into the tiny compartment as though it were Cinderella's glass slipper, praying it will fit just right. But some pieces of luggage are too obvious for words. A guitar is not overhead compartment compliant. On any airline!

My biggest pet peeve, however, is the armrest-hog. You know the guy; yes, it's always a guy. The passenger who sits next to you and assumes that it's okay not only to take over the armrest but to lean his arm on yours for support, using it as a cushion. You give him a polite nudge back. He pretends to readjust himself but soon takes even more space than before. You don't want to get irate and have to be escorted off the plane by security upon arrival, so what do you do?

Here are a few options I came up with during my last flight. If you are sitting in the middle or window seat, make frequent trips to the bathroom. Make him pay for that armrest. Or start sneezing and coughing – use a little spit every now and then. Make weird hacking noises to clear your throat.

Then, wipe your hands on the armrest as you make your way to one more trip to the bathroom. The ideas are endless; just think of all of the annoying passengers that have crossed your path.

Here is one of my favorites: rest your head on his shoulder and start drooling; get comfy; cross your legs; then get a nervous twitch; jiggle your foot. Oh, and don't forget to go to the bathroom again.

And if none of these suggestions work, tell your husband to change seats with you.

Bon voyage.

# Dear Alexander Hamilton

*By Robert McLoughlin*

My Uncle Jim has told me
That you and I are kin
You lived a brief but fruitful life
Til Aaron did you in

But Uncle Jim could be all wrong
His mind is very hazy
He lives in Marcy hospital
They say that he is crazy

But let's say Uncle Jim is right
We share a family tree
There is a limb where you abide
And there is one for me

But let's not brag my cousin dear
That we are on those limbs
For if you are my relative
You're also Uncle Jim's

# Cowboy State of Mind

*By Christopher Britton* ————————————————

He'd lived on a ranch
Through his formative years;
He'd roped and he branded
And put tags on cows' ears.

He'd earned his first callous
Before he was six,
Helpin' with fences
In need of a fix.

He'd been wind-burned
And sun-burned all of his life,
He could handle a rifle
And skin with a knife.

He'd been butted and kicked
And bitten and throwed,
But never gave it much thought
'Cause it was all that he knowed.

He'd considered his schoolin'
Jest one job like another.
So he did real well,
And that pleased his mother.

The few things he said,
Though he mostly stayed mum,
Tended to make others
Look up to him some.

But he didn't much care
Fer sittin' in class,
An' when it came time fer college,
He decided to pass.

He wanted to make his livin'
By usin' his hands –
Ridin' and ropin'
An' workin' the land.

But his folks just insisted
That he get a degree,
And they turned a deaf ear
To his every plea.

So on his eighteenth birthday
He found himself sittin'
In class at a college
He was thinking of quittin'.

But a funny thing happened
Before he cut himself loose.
He met this pretty blond gal,
And got caught in her noose.

She was smart; she was funny;
She was a great kisser,
And he knew if he quit,
How much he would miss her.

But she'd growed up in a city.
Her dad was a judge,
An' she was poison on ranchin'
An' just wouldn't budge.

"Ranching's unreliable,"
She said with some rancor.
"You spend most of your life
Kissing' up to some banker.

"When you have lots of cows,
The market goes 'poof';
Then when you have none,
It skies through the roof.

"You like living outdoors
Sleeping under the stars
But you're only eighteen
And you're covered with scars!

"You have a knee that won't work right
From being bucked off at a fair,
And your ear's a bit ragged
Where you were chewed by that mare.

"In the winters you freeze
Feeding cows in a blizzard,
An' if you're not careful, in summer,
You'll get bit by some lizard.

"Now I'm not gonna tell you
How your life you must run,
But if you have any brains,
You'll re-think your fun."

He brought her home fer a visit,
Hopin' she'd change,
But when she found a tick in her hair,
She was done with the range.

Meanwhile in classes,
He was doin' okay.
He jest didn't have it in him
To pull less than an "A".

Between bein' so smart
And this pretty gal's urging
His resolve to go ranching
He slowly was purging.

He wrote to his folks,
"I know you'll think me a fool,
But I guess I've decided
To go to law school."

Well, imagine their dismay
That the source of their pride
Turned his back on the ranch
And went to the dark side!

They didn't say nuthin'.
They just smiled and nodded,
Though fer his pa to be gracious,
He had to be prodded.

Of course, he married the gal.
She knowed he'd go far,
And she gentled down some
After he passed the bar.

So the boy now a man
Took up the law,
Which to his great surprise
Filled him with awe.

He was arguin' cases
All over the West,
An' before too much time passed
He'd become one of the best.

He still didn't say much;
His words they were few,
But those he did speak,
You knew they were true.

He was night herdin' books now,
Rounding up cases,
Mending broke laws
In all sorts of places.

Twenty years passed.
He'd become a big man in town,
When a reporter happened to ask him
To what he owed his renown.

"Well, one thing," he replied,
That got me off to my start
Was the love of my wife,
Who played a big part.

"I had my heart set on ranchin';
It was the way I was raised,
But she was dead set against it;
Said I was 'crazed.'

"Then I discovered hard work's
Hard work, whatever the place,
Whether you're deliverin' a calf
Or tryin' a case."

" 'Listen to nature,'
My dad always said,
'Cause the more you can hear it,
The less chance you'll be dead.'

"An' what's true on the prairie,
Also wins cases.
Talkin's important,
But listenin' is aces.

"People can be fractious
Just like bulls and horses,
If you're going to gentle 'em down,
You got to use your resources.

"Ya gotta keep yer eyes and ears open,
Even while you are duckin',
And try to understand what it is
That made 'em start buckin'."

"Once you got it figured
Why folks are squawkin',
Only then is the time
When you oughta start talkin'."

Having said all of this,
He leaned back in his chair,
Chewed on his lip
With a thousand yard stare.

"No day goes by," he went on,
"When some such lesson I learned
Don't come back to help me
Avoid gittin' burned.

"Bein' a cowboy
Ain't jest chaps and a rope.
It's about solvin' problems
An' never givin' up hope.

"When you've been raised on the range,
I think that you'll find,
That the way of the cowboy
Forever dwells in yer mind."

# No – No – No Abby

*By Shelly Burdette-Taylor* ——————————

Before sunrise on a Saturday morning
Mama and Papa need to work
Abby comes to the rescue to care for Adonis

Enter the main room to find Mama with Adonis on her lap quietly,
watching Blues Clues and sipping on water

Instructions are –
DO NOT Disturb Him for one full hour

He crawls into my lap
Cuddle and wait, cuddle and wait…
Right before the full hour
Start the tickle game and the horns – da – da – da – da

He slithers off my lap
Points his "…little, fat, right, index finger" and says…

No – No – No Abby

Been Told

# Living at Walmart

*By Mary Carnes*

I'M on my way to my local Walmart to print some pictures I have in my camera. It's about 10:30 on a warm morning in May. Because I don't want to hang around inside the store for any longer than I need to, I plan to use the digital photocopier that costs a few cents more but produces instant prints.

At the photo center, the woman ahead of me in line is wearing a plaid knee-length skirt, white blouse and ordinary black-laced shoes. On her head is a cap/scarf that identifies her as a modern-day nun.

She looks back and smiles at me. I return the smile and wait patiently while she puts picture after picture on the screen for copying. Finally, I can't wait any longer and leave to do some shopping. When I return, the nun is still there doing the same thing. I wait a little longer, then, frustrated, leave the store, vowing to return another time.

In fact, I return more than once during that week, arriving in the morning or afternoon, and on different days. On each occasion I have other things to buy in the store, but mainly I want my pictures printed. And each time, there's that same nun in front of the digital photocopier I want to use.

I begin to think that perhaps she lives at Walmart. Of course, I don't really believe this – not until I find an article on the Internet about a sophomore college student by the name of Skyler Bartels, who did just that – lived at a Walmart store in Des Moines, Iowa.

\* \* \*

Columnist Marc Hansen of the *Des Moines Register* wrote the story, and Bartels got quite a bit of publicity out of it. The student, a writing major from Drake University, said, "I'm not out to get anyone. I just thought it would be an interesting sociology experiment as a school project." He planned to spend his entire spring break at the store, but was caught on the third day.

"Some kids go to Cancun," Hansen wrote, "Skyler Bartels went to the Garden and Patio Department."

Bartels wanted to find out if Walmart really could "meet his every need, twenty-four hours a day," as their television ad suggested.

He went into the store wearing jeans and a white T-shirt, carrying only his cell phone for emergencies, his heart medicine, two forms of identification, and his debit bankcard. Deciding not to buy anything he couldn't carry around in the store, he ended up with a jacket (for storage space), a note pad, pencils, an electric voice recorder, a three-pack of underwear, a comb, toothbrush and toothpaste.

He lived on energy drinks, doughnuts, yogurt and Subway sandwiches, and he even paid to get his hair washed and shampooed at the Walmart Salon. Bartels figured he slept four hours out of the forty-one he spent in the store. "The best place for dozing," he said, "was at the Lawn and Garden where the lights weren't so bright and the furniture was comfortable."

The college student pretended to be looking at merchandise when the salespeople and stockers were around. "The worst part," he said, "was the one-to-four A.M. shift where it was hard to blend in."

During one day-shift he met a military recruiter who told him "he had what it took." The columnist had to ask

Bartels what that meant since the scruffy-looking kid had long hair, a slender build, and a beard.

He said, "I had good posture and didn't look sad."

While at the store, he met a nun, Sister Mary Sue, and even took a picture with her. I just knew there had to be a nun in the story!

By the third day the employees were suspicious, but when caught, Skyler Bartels was not arrested or charged with any crime. However, Walmart's corporate spokesperson, Sharon Weber, emphasized, "We're a retailer, not a hotel."

So, it only made sense to me that the nun I encountered over and over again at the Walmart on Murphy Canyon Road in San Diego had to be living in the store, too, just like that student – sleeping on the furniture, and reproducing picture after picture after picture.

# Smile, Sarah

*By Jeff Curtiss Welch*

"LOOK, I really like this but..." Her voice trails off. She kicks pebbles with the toes of her sneakers as she rocks slightly on the swing.

"Yes, sweety?" I sit in the swing next to her.

"Well..." She looks at her shoes. A huge sigh takes over her small frame. "This every other Saturday is crap."

"Oh, Sarah, that's –"

"I get that you and Mommy are separated or whatever, and ... I should be happy she lets me see you at all."

"Is everything okay at home?"

"Yeah." She shrugs. "I guess." Her feet move faster, rolling the gravel beneath them.

"School?" I prompt.

"The same."

"That's good, right? You still have your friends."

She looks at me suddenly. "She took down all the pictures of you!"

"Oh." Taken aback, I have no quick response.

"The ones from Disneyland. You and me at the beach." Her blue eyes are fading, filling with tears.

"Um." I tread lightly. "It might be painful to be reminded."

"But I want to be reminded." She sniffs and her voice catches. "It's startin' to feel," she squeaks, "like those things never happened!"

Last summer is a long time ago for an 8-year old. I kind of understand. I'm the child of divorce. And I'd sworn never to do that to any children of mine. But things started going south when Sarah learned to talk. She wanted to go everywhere I went. That wasn't possible. My job took me out of town more and more. And, consequently, I'd come home to "Daddy!" followed by "Your daughter's been insufferable."

The trinkets I brought back satisfied one of them. Abby's "hrumph" and glare said, "You went all the way to Charlotte and all you brought me is this cheap mug?"

Like I had any time for shopping after 10 to 12 hours on site, collapsing like a ragdoll at the hotel. The required early arrival at airports afforded me at least a few minutes at the over-priced shops beyond TSA. There were always stuffed animals adorned in "I ♥" tee-shirts. Sarah added each to her collection, and a new pushpin to her wall map indicating the city of ♥.

Everything boiled over after my longest trip – two-and-a-half weeks in Japan. I made the mistake of commenting on the mini-skirted, black-haired, porcelain-skinned Japanese women one too many times.

Abby exploded. "Maybe you should've brought one back for your daughter's collection."

On Friday night, after my first day back to work from the trip, I arrived home to find my suitcase and several large black trash bags on the front porch. A note on the door read, "Go to a hotel. Don't call me." I heeded the message, imagining – no, hoping – she'd cool down over the weekend. I didn't even attempt my key in the door; I didn't want to find out for sure if she'd changed the locks.

As I backed out of the driveway, I could see a little head silhouetted between the window and the curtains. She didn't wave. Nor did I.

That was two months ago. Two months for me; a seeming eternity for her.

"Sarah?"

Her scrunched-up face softens. She loves to hear me say her name.

I try to make my voice as soothing as possible. "We need to give Mommy some space."

She cocks her head. "Space?"

"Give her some time. I need to –"

"You *need* to come back home. It's your house. Our house."

"Sarah, I..."

"No. Come back home." Her brows furrow. "Daddy, Momma's not happy with you gone."

"I think you're –"

"No!" She crosses her arms. "Mommy's not happy." She looks at the space in front of her. "I know. She's not happy." She shoots me her glance. "Are you?"

"Well, of course not, honey. I'm away from you." I muster a smile.

She turns up the corner of her mouth. "You've been away from me plenty. On your trips. But your stuff was always there. I knew you were coming back."

I stare at my shoes. Her angry insistent eyes make me want to cry.

For the last few years, Abby and I had drifted apart. The newness of everything had grown stale. Abby wanted to rejoin the workforce, but we were wary of a stranger basically raising our child. Yet, each month left her further out of the technological loop. She even began to comment about the "younger kids" coming out of school with more knowledge than she. "And they don't know yet what's truly impossible." She tried working from home, but missed the social interaction.

I sigh and prepare myself for Sarah's counter-logic. "Sweety," I say looking right at her, like an adult not my loving daughter. "Your mother and I have a few things to work out."

Her mouth begins to draw into a frown.

I head off her comment. "It's not over, Sarah. We haven't talked about divorce yet."

"*Yet?*" Her eyes grow wide, wet.

"No, that word hasn't come up." I reach out and run my index finger under her chin. "It's not 'over.' "

"You said 'yet.' " Her bottom lip begins to tremble.

"My mistake, sweetheart. Slip of the tongue." I stick my tongue through my teeth.

She almost smiles. "Okay..." she says warily.

"You know, I have to change some things. Your mother wants to go back to work."

"I know. That's okay."

My hand moves to cup the golden curls behind her ear. "So you understand?"

"Yeah. Tammy's mom works. And Lindsay's."

"You want to swing some more?"

"No. I think our time's about up."

We walk the four blocks to the house, hand in hand, not speaking.

Just as Sarah puts her key to the lock, the door opens. Abby lets Sarah pass.

"George, we need to talk."

I feel my shoulders slump, my gaze drop.

"George? George, look at me."

I do.

"I had an interview this week. They just called. Yeah, on a Saturday. They want me to start as soon as possible." She grabs my hand and presses a new golden brass key onto my palm. "You need to come home." She almost smiles. Behind her, in the kitchen doorway, Sarah does.

Abby's arms reach for my shoulders. "Let's work this out."

Sarah's arms wrap around our legs. "Yes, Daddy."

# Utopia Ubetcha

*By Robert McLoughlin*

I live in San Diego
A perfect place for me
I can munch my taco
Where desert meets the sea

The people here are friendly
Most came from other places
I think that they are happy
You can see it on their faces

The sun shines here 'most every day
And gentle breezes blow
It doesn't rain too often
And you'll never see it snow

The curse we have is earthquake
Let's make that bummer halt
When you ask me who's to blame
It's San Andreas' Fault

I shall live in San Diego
Until the day I die
Am I a fool to trade this home
For some place in the sky

# Hi Tech, Bye Simple

*By Erika Toraya*

THE world is inundated with technology that is supposed to simplify my life. It's hard to live in the fast-paced, technology-run society that is taking over. Slowly but surely, this war strategy, under the guise of helpful advancement, has blind-sided some, but not me. It is a well thought out plan of intelligent, scheming people to dominate the world with their programs, software upgrades, and technological creations. With a new app here and a touch-tap there, here a pad, there a pod, everywhere a new fad 'gadg'.

Simplicity seems to have given way to billionaire programmers gifting us with games that deprive us of face-to-face interaction. Sharing our lives is now about tagged photos on-line for the world to see instead of private conversations and photo albums over coffee. Some of us still live with the waning hope of being helped on the phone by a human and paying bills with checks.

The biggest hassle for me is incurred by the security system that keeps me out of my own information. My list of passwords is about 55 long. And that isn't even all of them, since at the time I created some, I thought, "No problem. I'll remember this one. No need to write it down." That's great until it's time to open my secured site and find what I thought I remembered is wrong. Now I'll waste fifteen minutes or more creating a new password, not to mention the major mental anguish connected with supplying the username, account number and other information each site requires.

Passwords, people say, are easy if you just keep them all the same. Not so, not so. Some require eight characters, others demand a numeric symbol or capital letter. Don't make it 'weak' or common. Think of something unique from the other millions of online customers. And don't even dare use consecutive numbers or letters.

Oh my gosh, are we really concerned that people will hack into our personal Travelocity account or our Time Warner bills? Or maybe someone wants to pay my mortgage this month or see who I know on LinkedIn. No, it's a conspiracy to weed out those of us who are not technology-savvy when we must log in to our Facebook, email, health insurance, credit cards, as well as entertainment websites for sports, videos and music, just to name a few. We will give up and slowly fade away.

The techies are waiting for me to give up hope, when I can't remember my "username" and "password." Is my user name my account number or my name? Did I capitalize it? Did I put a space? Because you know it won't work if there is a space that doesn't belong. Oh, and I must prove it's me. Okay, that shouldn't be too hard, since I am me. But, which question do they ask me as proof? My childhood best friend? I have to think that far back? Or the obscure, "Your father's best friend's teacher's dog's name."

So, I pass the secret answer test. Next is the encoded temporary password with symbols written upside down on top of each other masked behind lines and characters that must have been created on another planet. And it has the audacity to say, "We must know you are a human." The computer is testing me to see if I am human?

Two tries later I am deemed human and allowed to create a new password. Write it down so I won't forget and have to go through all of this again. Shoot, was it capitalized? Ugggg!

# The Wave

*By Dave Schmidt*

The wave rises upon the ocean
A high point in a state of happiness
Only to diminish in the briefest motion

Next down to the trough of the wave
A low point in boredom or indifference
Yet to rise up again with feeling to save

Back to the top of the wave once more
Another high point in sadness or sorrow
Next to fall off and repeat forevermore

Occasionally the wave settles down, with less motion
Such a contrast to experience peacefulness
With forces at play, not long before a restless ocean

At long last the wave merges into the sea
Now in perpetual delight, state of ever-new joy
First four mental states recede, now the fifth a Reality

# Just Flowers

*By Jeff Curtiss Welch*

"THEY'RE not 'just flowers', sir," said the woman behind the counter. "*These* are 'please forgive me for forgetting until moments ago it's our special day' flowers." She waved her hands over them as if incanting. Her eyes were fixed on mine; but they looked *into* me.

"And how do you –" I started to ask.

"I *know*, sir." The shop seemed to get darker, a faint light coming from the vase.

I had to blink and look away; she was freaking me out. "I was thinking –"

"Not roses, sir. Roses won't work this time."

I was gazing at her again, but didn't remember turning. I shook my head to break whatever spell she'd cast. "No, no. She *likes* roses. They're her fav–"

"Not today. You've used them too many times before. Her unblinking eyes with the near-black irises drew me in again as I attempted to step back. "*These* are guaranteed."

"Guaran–"

"Trust me, sir."

"Well," I started. "If you –"

"I do."

I reached for my wallet. At this late hour, I had no time to go anywhere else.

"Cash only, please," she said in the same level tone.

I put three twenties on the counter, even though I didn't know the cost. "And if these don't –"

"They will." She took the money and placed it in a box next to her. "Guaranteed." She turned and disappeared behind a bead curtain.

I felt released. With trembling hands, I shuffled to the door clutching the warm emerald vase.

"Treat them gently, sir," came her faraway voice.

I set them on the passenger seat, then pulled the seatbelt across them.

Arriving home, I left my briefcase in the car. As I reached for the knob, hugging my purchase to my chest, the door swung open. My wife's face was pulled back in a smirk.

"Here," I said, holding out the vase. "For you, Sweety. Happy anniversary."

As soon as her hands touched the green glass, her icy stare melted and her mouth opened.

"They're −" She blinked. "Lovely." She drifted into the dining room and placed the vase on the table between two unlit candles. A small package wrapped in glittering red foil sat at my place.

"The good china," I mumbled.

"But of course." She swung around and threw both her arms around my neck. After planting a hard kiss on me, she said, "I made your favorite. Now go wash up."

I trudged to the bedroom and kicked off my shoes as I always did; only tonight, I set them inside the closet. I took off my jacket and hung it up. Instead of going to dinner in my undershirt, I went into the bathroom to straighten my tie.

The man in the mirror looked more like the guy she'd dated than the one I'd become. He wasn't jowly and graying; he was a young, vibrant newlywed.

When I poked my head into the kitchen, she purred, "Go sit down. It'll just be another minute."

I sat and stared at the small package. I so wanted to open it, a child-at-Christmas excitement in my chest.

"Hope you're hungry." She sailed through the doorway with a serving platter in one hand and a large salad bowl in the other. She placed them on the table, then leaned over to kiss the top of my head. As she moved to her place, I sprang from my chair to pull out hers.

"Thanks, Honey." She giggled.

I put my hand on the back of her neck and gave her rouged cheek a peck. She turned her head, giving me a ruby red kiss on the lips. Tingles went down my spine; I felt weak-kneed.

"Mmm," she whispered. "Let's eat now."

When I sat down, her deep brown eyes reached across the table. "I love you," sprang from my mouth.

"Oh, Ted," she squealed. "And I love you." She leaped from her chair and flew around the table. Pushing her face into mine, she kissed me like she hadn't done in years.

When she returned to her place at the table, I noticed the red foil-wrapped box was gone.

# Why Write? Why I Write

*By Robert Ross*

*The role of a writer is not to say what we can all say, but what we are unable to say.* — Anaïs Nin, American author

WHY WRITE? On October 20, 2014, The National Council of Teachers of English will be holding the fifth annual National Day on writing. According to the NCTE website, this annual day is set aside to celebrate composition in all its forms, encourage diverse participants – students, teachers, parents, grandparents, service and industrial workers, managers, business owners, legislators, retirees, and many more to celebrate writing in all its forms.

To the question, "Why write?", some of last year's participants penned: "Because I am a spider and words are my silk." And, "To get 10 years worth of stories out of my head." One person wrote, "Because I sound smarter when I write than when I speak." Another "Because saying words is nice, but writing them down lasts longer." And, "Because I'm in love." Or, "To think, to converse, to express, to solve, to explain, to persuade, to motivate, to…"

There are as many reasons to write as there are reasons to speak, to laugh, to cry, to be. Descartes' famous quote: "I think, therefore I am," could easily be restated, or in this case, rewritten to: "I write, therefore I am." In all of us is the desire, the drive, and the need to express ourselves. It's in our DNA. For some, that need to express, to share, comes out through writing.

Writers are a special breed for they live multiple times. In her book. *Writing Down the Bones*, Natalie Goldberg penned: "Writers live twice. They go along with their regular lives, are as fast as anyone in the grocery store, crossing the street, getting dressed for work in the morning. But there's another part of them that they have been training. The one that lives everything a second time. That sits down and sees their life again and goes over it. Looks at the texture and the details."

## Why I Write

Growing up in a house of seven was challenging for me. I was one of 5 children, in the middle, more introverted than extroverted. Life, as far back as I can remember, was an ongoing challenge to find peace and quiet, to reflect, to be me. However, there were the continual admonishments from parents, older siblings and teachers: "You shouldn't say that." "That's not nice." Be this way. Be that way. Do this. Do that. Stand. Sit. Be quiet. Go. Stop. And one that I heard more than a few times, "Go to the principal's office!" I was emotionally pummeled from all sides and didn't know it, surviving this onslaught by going inwards, not sharing, shutting down.

It wasn't until my mid-twenties that I discovered writing. I could write something without an older sister or a parent telling me what I should or shouldn't say. It was a new found freedom. My introspective thoughts put on paper, examined, rearranged to find my truth. A relationship, an experience, a feeling, a lover, was now fuel for pen and paper. So I wrote and wrote and wrote and wrote: poems, prose, and scribblings. Mostly unshared writings, but it didn't matter, they were my thoughts, mine alone. I felt like a child first learning to walk; exploring the landscape of the heart, the depth of the soul, through writing.

The Berkeley Free Press published my first article in 1974, about working with migrant farm workers in Oregon. It was exhilarating to see my thoughts in a Bay area newspaper. The stilted, shy, repressed kid of the past was now able to speak, to say what was on his mind, to share, through writing.

Writing was my way of communicating with the outside world. In the mid 90's, the angels of writing smiled down on me. I landed a steady assignment as a columnist for an Orange County magazine. I could now do, on an ongoing basis, what writers do: write, relive, explain, learn, and reexamine life's experiences. And most important, I could declare, on paper, in words, in my words: *hey, this is me!*

And so I wrote with a focus and purpose. I wrote about trips and observations and current events. I wrote about 9-11, the financial crisis, the war in Iraq. I opened the doors to my personal life and wrote about painful events, the death of my father and the day cancer showed up on our doorstep.

The cancer piece was the most difficult I had ever written. My wife, Ingrid, had a 7-centimeter sarcoma tumor. The news of the cancer began as a light rain, but quickly turned into a tsunami that crashed its way into my home leveling every sense of normalcy in its path. Uninvited, hell had arrived.

Eventually, after the surgeries and radiation, I picked up the pen to relive and reexamine the process, again feeling the helplessness while watching her go through some very painful days. Reliving the afternoon and evening of the first surgery. Reflecting on the act of praying, even though I wasn't affiliated with any religion and had never prayed a day in my life. The writing brought it all back; the emotions, raw, and at times overwhelming.

But, 'looking at the texture, the details,' also revealed some silver linings to the cancer experience; the flowers on the doorstep from caring friends, food dropped off to bring comfort, the get-well cards, and the concern from family members. People cared. Cancer involves more than one. The title of the column: When Cancer Knocks, Everyone Answers.

I don't know where this writing life is going. My friends, paper and pen, will be with me though. I'll push the envelope a bit, look for new ways to say the same old things, peel off an emotional layer or two, perhaps explore new forms of writing. And, I'll keep Franz Kafka's thoughts on writing always in mind: "Don't bend; don't water it down; don't try to make it logical; don't edit your own soul according to the fashion. Rather, follow your most intense obsessions mercilessly."

October 20, 2014, is the National Day on Writing; a day to reflect, and ask: why write?

# Searching for Security

*By Nancy Foley*

ONE of the most overworked words in our current vocabulary might be security. *Financial security, job security, airport security, national security, border security, social security, school security, home security, food security, internet security, security locks and gates, security guards,* and let's not forget, *security blanket.*

Webster defines security as: freedom from danger, risk, anxiety; something that protects, shelters, or makes safe; precautions us against crime or attack.

Every morning, whether on TV, radio, online, or in newsprint, we are informed of another breach of security on the global, national, or local level. The media and their advertisers constantly bombard us with reminders to purchase "cutting edge" security devices in every price range. But can we ever feel completely secure? When did we become insecure about security?

As I observe the daily routine of my seven grand-children and reflect upon the early years of my four children, I wonder if human beings have felt completely secure since leaving the womb.

My grandchildren live in a safe environment with high-tech, child-proof furnishings and toys. Yet, when they become fussy or tired, they grab their favorite blanket, stuffed animal, or pacifier. Do these objects bring them comfort because they feel insecure?

Josh, the oldest at seven years, still clings to a frog that was originally green with long velvet arms and legs. Now one arm is missing, its color has changed to gray, and it has a pungent odor despite multiple washings. But "Ahby" gives Josh the comfort he needs, his sense of security.

His brother Patrick, who is four years old, drags around a heavy, hand-knitted blanket, and has yet to part with his pacifier at night. He suffers from asthma and allergies. So despite his age, his parents allow him to continue using his "pacy" for comfort.

Lucy was visited by the "beebe" fairy when she turned four. The fairy took all of her pacifiers to give to newborns in less fortunate neighborhoods. Her eyes showed concern as she asked her mommy and daddy, "Is there a blanket fairy too?" Her favorite pink blanket, although in shreds, stays under her pillow to cuddle with at bedtime. In addition, she has a night light and falls asleep listening to a CD of inspirational hymns.

Lucy's cousin, Zach, gave up his pacifier on his fourth birthday but still is consoled by a well-worn blanket, the same one that his mother used as a toddler. His cousins, Charlie and Jamie, both two years old, prefer thin gauze blankets. But Jamie also is soothed by a pacifier and a yellow furry duck that he calls "Quack".

Mackenzie, our youngest at eighteen months, has several favorite blankets but also sucks her thumb when she feels tired or upset.

As I recall the infant and toddler stages of our own children, I realize that all four of them experienced this same search for security. Erin sucked on a pacifier to help her fall asleep. When she turned three, we conveniently lost "pipey" and all of us endured several sleepless nights.

Katie underwent hernia surgery at three months and then again at three years. She clung to not one, but two security blankets. They were pink cotton thermal blankets with no bindings. These eventually evolved into her imaginary friends "Chiny and Quatty." When Katie was irritated or had an attention-getting tantrum, she retreated to her room and found comfort in the arms of her two blanket buddies. After she married and started removing personal items from her bedroom closet to take to their new home, I spied the pair of faded pink blankets peeking out of one of the boxes.

Tim never reached for a pacifier or a blanket. Instead, being a child who always entertained himself, he found comfort and bliss in sucking his two fingers, middle and ring, never thumb or pointer. He didn't latch onto a favorite blanket. However, after growing out of the finger-sucking stage, he found it difficult to fall asleep. Insecurity perhaps?

Our youngest, Sheila, clung to a soft yellow blanket with a smooth, satin binding. We were concerned when she wasn't talking at two years old. Friends reminded me that she didn't need to say anything because everyone gave her whatever she wanted. And because of all the chatter in our household, she probably never had a chance to speak.

Sheila dragged her blanket around the house, and, after several years, all that was left was the frayed binding. I have a vivid memory of her first day of kindergarten. I dropped her off at school, returned home, and opened the door. There at the threshold, curled up like a kitten, was her precious strip of satin beaming at me with love.

But all these symbols of security that we clung to as toddlers are considered inappropriate as we mature. I experience insecurity every time I board an airplane and, especially, when I'm home alone at night. Sometimes I wish I could still snuggle with the thin, nubby-white, sheet-size blanket that was my security as a child. I remember holding a corner of this "nunny" between my thumb and forefinger and rubbing it softly against my nose.

Helen Keller, world renowned author and founder of a non-profit organization devoted to preventing blindness, believed "Life is either a daring adventure or nothing. Security does not exist in nature, nor do children of men as a whole experience it. Avoiding danger is no safer in the long run than exposure."*

The German psychologist Erich Fromm wrote, "The task we must set for ourselves is not to feel secure, but to be able to tolerate insecurity."**

American motivational speaker and author Brian Tracy stated, "The more we seek security, the less of it we have."**

World War II General Douglas MacArthur wrote, "There is no security on this earth, only opportunity."**

We can spend our entire lives searching for the security that we may have felt only in the womb. My Christian faith teaches me that the search for complete security will not end until we take our last breath and enter the Kingdom of God. We will have no need for security blankets. There, at last, we will be safe, wrapped in the loving arms of our Heavenly Father.

"In peace I shall both lie down and sleep, for you alone, O Lord, make me secure." (Psalm 4:9)***

  * www.goodreads.com/quotes/tag/security
  ** www.ranker.com/list/notable-and-famous-security-quotes
*** New American Bible, St. Joseph Edition, 1991

# Sweet Memories

*By Jene Alan*

A Bob Dylan song played, "Lay lady lay, lay across my big brass bed. Whatever colors you have in your mind ... kaleidoscope of colors you will find."

His skin was dark, his smile was warm. His lips were the softest I've ever kissed. The man was delicious. We'd met at a friend's party and danced. As he dipped me low, I relaxed completely. He could pull me up again, but my knee went limp! He carried me over to a couch and massaged my knee gently. His hands were healing. He was a San Diego Charger, First string, tight end. 6'2", 260 pounds of muscle and energy. And when he focused on me, I saw a kaleidoscope of colors.

\* \* \*

"Your kisses send me to Shangri La. Each kiss is magic..." I've never been to Shangri La, but I have been to a great jazz bar in La Jolla, to listen to music, have a glass of wine and look around. A man approached me as I was leaving, and I certainly liked what I saw. He told me I had the most gorgeous legs he'd ever seen and asked if I'd like to go out sometime. Good looking guy, 6'2" with striking blue eyes. I gave him my number.

His specialty was oral sex. He was an expert on making love to a woman. He played me like a Stradivarius and I saw all the colors of the kaleidoscope in my soul.

# Does She Feel Me?

*By Wallace Watson*

In the mirror
I see my face and recognize my soul
Gentle and hopeful
Thoughts race through my head

Should I tickle her face?
Her third eye
With great hope
Above her I embrace

Hoping not to wake her
I move my energy
In a circular motion
Faster and faster

All my might and being
Focus on a spot above her nose
A million times faster
I push energy round and round

She opens her eyes
And says
It feels like someone
Tickled my third eye

# Winter Flight North

*By Jean E. Taddonio*

Clouds are serious here
dark billowing beauties on a mission
fill me with energy, sense of purpose

A parched earth waits like a thirsty writer
in the midst of drought
seeking inspiration, exhilaration
a flood of ideas – or just one good rain

A stranger sits beside me
sharing a window
witnessing clouds
in their stormy costumes

We marvel together
at nature's loveliness
One drought has lifted

# Follow Your Gut

*By Rita Early*

I'VE always been fascinated by foreign cultures and languages. In junior college I wanted to sign up for Elementary Chinese, but my counselor persuaded me to take Spanish 101instead.

"I already speak Spanish," I protested.

"If you want to get into UCLA, you're going to need all the A's you can get."

I slumped back in my seat defeated.

"Look," he said, trying to cheer me up. "Take the easy A now, and once you get to Los Angeles, take whatever you want."

Two years later, I walked down the corridor of the English department at UCLA. I was going to talk to my professor about dropping his class on James Baldwin. "But why?" he asked, "You're doing so well."

I didn't give him the whole truth; I was too afraid he'd tell me to play it safe and stick to my required literature class and take Italian at a community college – after graduation. So, I told him half of the truth. "I'm carrying too many units. I won't be able to keep up by midterm."

He wished me the best of luck and signed my drop card.

My Italian professor had beautiful silky black hair and big brown eyes. She was so energetic and passionate about teaching Italian she almost seemed Italian. Signorina Rodriguez was actually from Puerto Rico. A Puerto Rican teaching Italian to a Mexican. *Surely a sign from God.*

Seventeen years later, I still recall nouns, verbs, and expressions well enough to tell the pharmacist across the counter, "Il mio stomago non e buono, molto formaggio." Which roughly translates to, "My stomach is no good, too much cheese."

"Laxante?" asks the pharmacist.

"Si, si." I nod in agreement, thrilled at having been understood yet bummed that laxative is the same in Italian as in Spanish.

He holds the box and starts speaking faster, "Tre volte ogni giorno. Una per la mattina, una per il pomeriggio e una per la notte. Vabene?"

"Uhm…" is all I manage to say as I process what I've just heard. Something about the number three, one morning, blah-blah-blah, one night. *Shoot! He's telling me the dosage.* Must be three pills a day: one in the morning, one in the afternoon, and one at night.

"Vabene?" he asks again.

"Si," I reply handing over the Euros. "Vabene." All good.

As I walk out of the pharmacy in Florence I feel a sense of vindication. I dared to follow my gut seventeen years ago. My gut was now eternally grateful.

# Masquerade

*By Nancy Foley*

What kind of a mask do you wear?

Does your disguise protect what you feel?

Does anyone out there even care?

What kind of a mask do you wear?

Can you remove the shield, do you dare?

Have you secrets you must conceal?

What kind of a mask do you wear?

Does your disguise protect what you feel?

# Vanity

*By Linda Smith* ————————————

When I let it go, my unruly,
curly, gray hair, wiry as a
Brillo pad, sticks out like
antennae reaching for reception.

"When are you gonna stop
coloring your hair, Mama?"

"Not … yet."
I wonder. How would it feel?

Am I afraid people will
stop saying, "You look younger than that."
Or, will I no longer feel young?

But, I love older people--
their humor, wisdom,
knowledge and experience

I love their stories
and photographs in black and white.

Maybe I *am* older people…

So, why my hesitation to
look the part?

Dunno.

In the meantime, I'll
let my daughter know,
if she ever needs
a gift idea for me,

A bottle of my
favorite color will do
just fine.

# Silly Words

*By Tim Calaway* ————————————————————

I hold your head as you drowse
After your long day.
I trace your curls across your cheek
Feather soft and cool.
I hum and sing those simple words, our song.
"Gooba, Gooba, Gooba."
Silly as they sound, they work their magic,
And you sleep smiling.

Like trying to catch the hummingbird
In a camera lens;
So quick, can't focus, flitting is its work,
I could not catch it.
That is how quickly you were gone.
No time to prepare
Slack-jawed and hurt, feelings and memory
Put away and forgotten, almost.

Gooba, Gooba, Gooba
Now they are just silly words.

# Ruins are Alive

*By Erika Toraya*

The place where he is born
swaddled and rocked
though poor and meek
they adore, seek

The place where his parents
grow and live
meet and marry
persevere, give

The road he travels
with friends to inspire
teach goodness, truth
their hearts feel like fire

The home of his friend
where he prays and sleeps
such normal needs but deeper peace
I sink to my knees

The room where they eat
what it must have been like
share in friendship
for one last time

The room where he waits
sentenced and bloody
faces his death
knowing pure agony

We stand, envision
dungeon of memory
my friend weeps
as the women who love him

Extreme events
once a path to friends
now a land mine
of humiliation, pain so intense

Once laughing, healing
teaching the people
now hatred, betrayal
fear and evil

Walk the same path
touch where he touched
see the sights
capture a glimpse

Live in this moment
here in this place
past transcends into present
divine grace

The place of His tomb
triumph, resurrection
thousands go see
many come to know

This place, your life
always by our side
no, You were not ruined
Praise God, You are Alive

# Night
*By Rebecca Johnson* ————————————

Scrambled memories shrouded in twilight

Under dark shimmering blue at sunset

A screech owl tucked inside a box

  scratches and claws

Sharp rustle when the wind sails through leaves

Gives fireflies the jitters

Hours crawl by in the dim dayless sky

I lie awake and wait for dawn's welcome light

# Ode to the Microbe

*By Susie Parker*

Microbe, microbe, we love you so

Without you, crops won't grow

Won't bloom, won't thrive

Won't even survive

We know you are very small

But, without you, no Life at all

From the biggest whale to the smallest flea

From the pansy to the redwood tree

All things on Earth are your home

You are never truly alone

Shall we join in praise and say,

Have a National Microbe Day?

# Moment of Joy

*By Nui Rehfuss*

IN late October, 2009 my parents and I planned a trip to the Park and Recreation areas of a nearby city called Lum Pum. Mother considered this place to be very special, beautiful and relaxing to visit.

We started our day early in the morning. I was anxious about driving, because the road is narrow with curves, mountains, and deep cliffs. Plus, it was the monsoon season, so the road was wet, slippery and known as a fatal accident road. But I managed to make my parents feel comfortable, and we enjoyed the scenic views along the way.

After an hour and a half we saw unique varieties of rain forest trees, ponds and lakes. My parents and I started walking to the ponds full of lotus plants. In that moment I felt free and connected with nature.

In our culture (I grew up as a Buddhist) the lotus represents purity of the body, speech, and mind. But lotus can be used for many different purposes. The lotus plants remind me of many things about my mother's cooking. She used lotus stems for salad or soup, leaves for wrapping the food and the roots for herbal medicine.

Lotus roots have been found to be rich in dietary fiber, vitamin C, potassium, B12 and magnesium. Lotus seeds are also commonly used for desserts and snacks. After spending time at the lotus pond, we walked toward the sculpture of Manora.

Manora is an art form native to southern Thailand. The performance is a body dance with slow movements and stops with still postures, and each posture is different. These dances emanated from India. While we were enjoying the view, my mother mentioned that Manora was one of her favorite entertainments.

Then we continued to walk away from the sculpture, crossed the small bridge to the Sa-La. The Sa-La is a picnic table, which is made of brick. The center pieces are decorated with shadow-play leather puppet characters. It is very impressive, and we took some pictures and relaxed before we continued to the other part of the park.

Shadow play, called "Nang Thalung" in Thailand, is a popular art form in the south. The shadow play picture is made of dried animal skin, painted with natural color plants. These are carved into drama figures like a hermit, a lord, a giant, etc. The shadow play is reserved for special holidays. My parents rarely missed a show if the play was not too far from home.

This trip was special and fulfilling for me to see my parents enjoy seeing their favorite places, having some relaxation and appreciating our culture. The pictures from this trip reward me with so many precious memories.

# If Only You Could See

*By Nancy Foley* ——————————————

He leaned back in the chair and said to me

If only you could see               what I hear

      Rushing streams in early spring

      Distant cry of the whippoorwill

      Wind whistling through autumn trees

      Faint chime of church bells at noon

If only you could see               fragrances I inhale

      Summer's new mown grass

      Luscious lilacs perfuming the air

      Spicy pine from Christmas tree lot

      Sweet breath of a newborn in my arms

If only you could see               delicacies that tickle my

taste buds

      Fresh mint in a frosted glass of tea

       A crunchy bite of newly picked corn

      Warm buttery home-baked biscuits

      Slushy ripe watermelon juice

If only you could see               what my fingers feel

Lacy snowflakes on a winter's morn

Dark moist soil for early planting

Slender throat of a calla lily

Her heart pulsing next to mine

If only you could see          the way I see.

# Our American

*By Tim Calaway* ─────────────────────

*One French family had tended for years the grave of a G.I.*
*who'd been hastily buried on their farm.*
> *The Noir Forties*, Richard Lingeman, p.49

Rest easy, Our American.
By your comrades long ago
You were left with us

You lie in our orchard
Under white blossoms in spring.
Safe now from harm

Our American, were you brave
Or scared when you fell?
No matter, for you were here for us.

Many years we have tended
That holy place on the hill
With thanks for what you gave.

And so it will be
Until all of this family
Rests along with you.

# What to Do About Julie

*By Donna Ferguson*

THE biggest of the upstairs closets was almost empty. Just two things remained: an oil painting of a priest by the name of Father Moynahan, and a plaster-of-Paris lawn statue of The Sacred Heart of Jesus.

"Hey, Wendell. What about these?"

Wendell Hennessey and I had been friends for more than forty years. Together, we had taken on the grim task of going through the possessions of the Heaney family, who had resided in the same house for more than three quarters of a century. My husband's Aunt Alice, the only Heaney left, had mentored Wendell, a neighborhood kid from up Maplewood Street, and steered him into the field of academics when he was a young man. He'd been visiting the old house and the women who lived there since he was twelve, some fifty years before.

"Aw, I don't want that stuff. I've been surrounded by it all my life. Get rid of it."

"Wendell, we can't just set Jesus out on the curb. I mean… Oh, fine. I'll take him with me to Susan's. But as to Father Moynahan, well, I never really knew him…"

"Yeah, I know what you mean. As I recall, Alice did that portrait of him in the late fifties, early sixties. Their association started when he brought communion to her mother, who, as you know, never set foot outside the house again after she broke her hip."

"Wasn't Father Moynahan a Jesuit?"

"No. But he had great intellect for a parish priest, something he had in common with Alice. I think I remember hearing he had a niece somewhere in the vicinity. Maybe I can track her down and give the painting to her…if she's not dead too."

"Good idea," I said. Problems solved. Well, at least two of the indeterminate number that kept bubbling up through the floorboards of late.

Alice had entered a nursing home three years before, at the age of 85. Prior to that Wendell had looked in on her – almost daily after her sister died – until her falls began, and home was no longer a safe environment. Payouts to the nursing home had depleted the family's liquid assets. The house would have to be sold. It was time.

Sorting through a living person's possessions is something akin to ransacking, only neater. Our responsibility to separate trash from treasure felt onerous and regrettable. We brought our growing list of concerns to a higher power, an $800-an-hour Boston attorney Wendell and I had consulted on Alice's behalf.

"The Heaney residence has been unoccupied for the past three years," I said. "Shouldn't we remove at least the valuables from the premises at this time?"

"Yes. But remember, you are custodians, only – curators actually, if the truth be told. In the event that Alice arises from her bed at the care center, and is discharged home, her possessions must be returned. They are hers, until she dies."

Wendell and I looked at one another and nodded. This was going to be a long, hot summer.

I had already been through this once before, when my mother was diagnosed with Alzheimer's and had to be moved to an assisted living facility. But Wendell had never cleaned out a house before; he lived in the home where he was born, and had no idea of all that it entailed.

"Let's begin with the obvious trash," I said.

"That should take care of most of the cellar," Wendell said.

"Now, now. Don't take anything for granted. You know as well as I do that Alice squirreled stuff away all over the place. Let's look carefully."

"I don't even want to think about that office upstairs," Wendell groaned.

"I know what you mean. There are so many books in there I can't even imagine where to start."

And so it began, a slow, laborious sifting, through drawer after drawer. Items that had stood vigil for decades on the now dusty shelves were cleaned, and inspected. Donation boxes overflowed with old manicure kits; plastic gadgetry from the bargain bin at Building 19; outdated make-up; hot water bottles, sleeping masks, silk scarves and stray garters. Cast-offs from a household, mostly female after World War II, when Alice's father died and her brother finally married to become my husband's stepfather.

The college classes Wendell taught would continue for several more weeks, so much of the sorting was left to me. Situations such as ours oftentimes got ugly when it came to the distribution phase, but fortunately, we trusted one another. Nothing in the house meant more to me than our long-standing friendship. Anything that looked to have value, sentimental, or otherwise, I put aside for Wendell's consideration.

Of the three tiny bedrooms upstairs, I slept in the largest, its walls hung with crucifixes and fading Norman Rockwell prints. I drifted off to sleep each night amidst forgotten mementos of European travel, and yet more dust that strangely enough, if undisturbed, didn't bother my allergies one bit.

Lacy, embroidered handkerchiefs spilled from a quilted satin box in one of the bureaus. Painstakingly hand-made, they represented a by-gone era. Another box contained gloves, dainty accoutrements of genteel femininity. I marveled at those things, preserved for special occasions, department store new but considered useless by our modern society. The top drawer of the Danish Modern dresser had become an inadvertent, twentieth-century time capsule.

One afternoon, I braved the heat in the upstairs office to go through a chest-of-drawers built into the eaves. Legs folded beneath me, I knelt down to examine the contents of each low drawer. In the middle one, nestled between some empty, silk-lined jewelry boxes was a square, hinged case, its velvet covering worn smooth by years of handling. That, plus the heft of it told me I was holding something unusual in my hand.

The velvet-lined interior housed a half-inch-thick, brass cylinder, with a diameter slightly larger than that of a silver dollar. In the center lay a dime-sized crystal-clear viewing port. When I brought it over to the window to peer through the opening, I recognized what was undeniably, a small piece of bone.

*A relic!* My sharp intake of breath broke the silence. "A first-class one, at that," I whispered aloud.

I'd learned long ago from Catholic friends that relics were divided into three categories. Third class relics were furniture, or implements that had touched something the venerated person had touched. Second class relics were most often clothing, burial shrouds, or things used every day that had touched the person's body. And first class relics were actual pieces of the saint, hair and bones, mostly. Tucked beneath the brass cylinder was a folded piece of paper, yellowed and disintegrating, which read:

> Prayer to obtain special favors through the
> intercession of Bl. Julie Billiart
> Blessed Julie, cured by your tender devotion to
> the Sacred Heart, and powerful even in life to
> gain your requests for others, obtain for us the
> special favors we now implore. Pater; Ave;
> Gloria. Pray for the canonization of Blessed
> Julie.

*Oh. So this was written when she'd been beatified, but hadn't graduated to sainthood yet.* Beneath the fragile paper was a clear piece of tape through which could be read: This relic should be returned to Rev. P.T.M. St. Bartholomew's, Everett.

*P.T.M... Hmmm. P.T.M.? Patrick Thomas Moynahan. Of course.* Though he'd died sometime in the early sixties, I'd heard that name mentioned repeatedly through the years. There were photos of him all over the house. He was tall, thin and unsmiling. Always wearing his cleric's collar.

*But how did the relic end up here? I must ask Wendell.*

"Oh, wow. Let me see that," Wendell said when I showed it to him that night. He turned the brass cylinder over in his hand. "I'll bet Father Moynahan brought this back from the Vatican."

"But, why would Alice have had it?"

"Many years ago she did extensive research about Julie Billiart, in preparation for writing a book. I'm pretty sure it was before she began teaching at B.U., and before St. Julie was canonized. Alice loved that St. Julie was a teacher, and felt a great kinship because they had both suffered prolonged illness and recovered. Father Moynahan may have given the relic to Alice when she was sick. Or perhaps, for literary inspiration, who knows?"

"Wow." I shook my head. "I can't decide whether the thing is creepy or not."

"Well, regardless, let's not lose track of it. I'll take it in case Alice would like to have it with her at the nursing home."

"Yeah, maybe she would." I nodded.

By the end of my stay, I had accumulated a collection of jewelry and household goods that Wendell assured me he couldn't use, but that I thought deserved to be saved from the donation pile. A couple of nights before I left, Wendell came down to help me divide up the art. My nerves were shot. We'd worked cooperatively thus far, but I knew the one thing that could make us lock horns would be Alice's paintings. I had admired them for the past forty years, and Wendell had been on hand when Alice was creating many of them. We went around the house and stopped before each painting. I held my breath and said, "How about this one."

"Nope." Wendell shook his head. "Take it."

"Are you serious? I've always loved that one."

"There's the one I want right there." I studied the painting he indicated and realized it was my least favorite.

And so it went. The moment I'd been dreading turned out to be the most gratifying of all. We claimed the works we had favored with absolutely no overlap. Both of us were amazed. It was much like the old New England saying, "There's an ass for every seat," which always makes me giggle.

That settled, I loaded up the station wagon I had borrowed from Susan and Steve, my friends in Westport, sixty miles southeast of Boston. I would be visiting them for a few days before heading back to California.

As I drove south along Route 24, Susan's voice poured from the Bluetooth gizmo affixed to my ear. "Well, of course you can store Alice's stuff here. There's that whole guestroom closet upstairs with hardly anything in it."

"Okay, but you'd better set another place at the table. I'm bringing a guest home with me tonight."

"Really? Who?"

I looked over at the statue belted into the passenger seat and said, "Jesus is my co-pilot – literally." Susan chuckled as I launched into my improvisation:

*I don't care if it rains or freezes,*
*Long as I got my plaster Jesus,*
*Ridin' in the front seat of my car.*

"Just be careful, you crazy woman. Jesus will have his hands full with those Boston rush-hour drivers cutting you off. I'll go up right now and clear the remaining stuff out of that closet."

\* \* \*

I traveled from California to the little house at the foot of Maplewood Street several times that year. I assisted Wendell with the huge task of assessing and categorizing items discovered in what we laughingly referred to as, "the other Big Dig." I grew used to city sounds, never fearful of the solitude the house offered, despite demographic changes in the neighborhood. Soft utterances of Brazilian Portuguese had begun to supplant the Italian dialects that had been heard in Everett for as long as most could remember.

Days were filled with the discovery, perusal, and packing of things that revealed secrets of generations of Heaney's: photos, needlepoint-pictures, decorative bric-a-brac. Plus a veritable battalion of saints, depicted in icons, carvings, statuary, and medals.

When we'd dealt with the last of it and the little house was ready for sale, I spent the final night in Everett at Wendell's home, the neat, two-and-a-half-story tenement he'd grown up in, at the top of Maplewood Street. The back porch balcony overlooked the Boston skyline with the most breathtaking view imaginable.

"Donna, there are a few more things you should go through before you leave." Wendell disappeared into another room and returned with a green satin zipper-bag. Inside were the oldest of the Heaney heirlooms: pocket watches, watch fobs, initialed gold brooches.

Some years before her death, Alice's younger sister had been diagnosed with kidney failure, and the little house was rife with caregivers. First a diamond ring went missing, then we discovered that a nurses' aide had used Alice's identity to set up a new cell phone account for herself. I advised Wendell at the time to take the most valuable heirlooms out of the house.

"Oh my goodness," I chuckled. "Here's Mrs. Heaney's gold watch that Alice accused me of stealing a few years back. I was so mad at her, I nearly died of apoplexy."

Wendell's grin lit up his face. "Then it's only fitting that you should have it, my dear."

"Hey, what about the relic?" I asked. "Not only was it orphaned by the death of Fr. Moynahan, but once the house sells, it'll be homeless too. What's to become of it, anyway?"

"I haven't mentioned it to Alice. Since her rings were stolen off her fingers while she slept, I'm reluctant to bring anything irreplaceable into the nursing home. Why? *You* want it?" Wendell's face registered surprise.

"Well, if you don't think my taking it home to San Diego will bring the plane down ... I'm not sure it's ever been handled by an Anglican before. When Julie was alive in the latter 1700's she'd have regarded me as a heretic, thanks to Henry VIII."

"True. But just think, Donna. If the plane goes down, you might be the only survivor because of it," Wendell said, with a twinkle in his eye.

"Okay, then." I nodded. "I'll take her."

As I walked toward airport security the next day I patted the outside of my voluminous travel handbag. *It's okay Julie. You're coming to live with me. You don't mind if I call you Julie, do you? I can understand if you would prefer St. Julie, though; I'm sure it took a lot of years to work up to that position.*

The rational, free-thinking part of me felt ridiculous lapsing into silent conversation with what was presumably a piece of someone's remains. But it wasn't just any bone. It had belonged to a person of note. Part of my fascination was the relic's age. Julie Billiart was born in 1751 and died in 1816 after having founded the Sisters of the Sacred Heart. *I hope you'll like it in California. We don't speak French there but there are plenty of Catholics, and it's warm. I'll bet you've never even seen a palm tree or the Pacific Ocean before.*

I'd always been captivated by holy statues, medals, and rosaries, mostly because they became the repositories of peoples' hopes and dreams. Held in sweating, shaking, or often hung-over hands, they received thanks as well as pleas for intercession or forgiveness. They heard confessions, comforted the sick, shielded the fearful, and were many times regarded as invisible friends by the lonely and aged.

After fastening my seatbelt, I thought back to December of 1961, when I was thirteen. My mother, sister and I were preparing to drive from Miami to Baltimore, to visit my brother Ben and his family, for Christmas. Earlier that year my father had died suddenly, of a heart attack. Four years before that, my other brother had been killed in a car accident. We'd never driven that far from home, and neither my sister nor my mother knew how to drive on snow or ice. The 1959 Pontiac we owned had no heater, no snow tires, and no seatbelts. I was scared shitless.

As we entered the car my mother was notably exasperated by the statue of the Blessed Virgin she found glued to the dashboard. Two pairs of eyes swiveled in my direction.

"Elmer's Glue-All. It's water soluble," I said.

Both my sister and my mother shook their heads at that, but neither removed the statue. She performed beautifully, by the way. We survived our frozen odyssey.

I'd bought the small plastic statue from the dime store a few weeks back, and discovered that the alcove of my bookcase headboard made a dandy little shrine.

"You're not even Catholic," my sister taunted. The tiny wreath of artificial flowers I'd placed around the head of the statue drove her nuts.

"I think she's pretty," I said, feeling the need to defend my purchase. What wasn't stated was that I was looking for protection. Any way I could get it.

St. Julie resided in the top drawer of my nightstand, once I got her home. But at intervals I found myself cracking the lid of the case, letting my hands warm the cool brass housing while I held it for a moment. Most times I thought it strange to be the caretaker of a two hundred year-old relic. But there were also moments when I wondered if it had been ordained.

The phone call about my ailing sister's condition came without warning, while I was out doing errands.

"Mummy isn't doing very well," my niece Karen said. "Says she's all done."

Never the crier, I sobbed all afternoon while packing for a cross-country flight. The last things I added: a black, three piece, Chico's ensemble and black leather heels.

Just before leaving for my red-eye flight to Pensacola, I stopped at the head of the stairs for a moment, and then returned to the bedroom. Not at all sure if it was a good idea, I opened the drawer and whispered through my tears, "I need you to come with me, Julie. We're heading out to a special assignment."

# First Snow

*By Harry Field*

The penitent night wind sobbed

Whispering her contrition.

Now, shriven at last,

The world wears a veil of purity.


Somber-habited pines, white-hooded,

Kneel like nuns before a crystal shrine,

And as the chalice of the sun rises,

Silently tell their rosaries,

Diamond beads dropping,

One by one.

# Grandma Nancy

*By Joe Torricelli*

Grandma Nancy thanks and kisses
From us the children – all your kids
You made the Congress pass a health bill
For us forever and they did

Kids without a loving grandma know
Care's what caring people give. A dying
Child's got a legal right to Treatment
The inalienable right to life.

# Minstrel Man

*By Cheri LaLone* ————————————

Minstrel man of winter lands

Sing me a song of mornings gone

Play me a tune of a time soon

When our spirits will share

The same summer's air


With you I share a passion rare

And pulses race a faster pace

Than I have known before


Come stay with me

Come pray with me

Make this marriage bond

For you will never find a soul

That blends as well as mine

# Reflections on Cuba

*By Robert Ross*

*A revolution is not a bed of roses. A revolution is a struggle between the future and the past.*     – Fidel Castro

CUBA is 'struggling.' It's struggling with a worn-out and unworkable revolutionary vision. Struggling economically, partly due to a U.S. imposed trade embargo and travel ban, and struggling with their own political identity in a world that has shrugged off the Communist ideology of the 1950's. As a result, visiting Cuba is like no other experience in the world.

In 1956 Fidel and Raul Castro, Che Guevara and a handful of revolutionaries land on a remote beach of Cuba. For three years, they fight the army of the brutal dictator Juan Batista. On January 1, 1959, revolutionary forces led by Fidel Castro enter Havana greeted by cheering mobs.

Initially, Fidel nationalizes some companies and land reform is put in place, giving title to two hundred thousand peasants. But, when Fidel reveals his true revolutionary vision, trying and executing as many as 500 former Batista officials within three months of taking power and nationalizing the bulk of private companies, America reacts. The door closes on relations. Simultaneously, the former Soviet Union, under Nikita Khrushchev, opens the door to Cuba, establishing trade relations and other forms of assistance, including military aid. Cubans exit the small island country in droves. The stage is set for a half-century drama that, at one point, brought the world to the brink of a nuclear catastrophe.

There are two ways for Americans to travel to Cuba: illegally, by going to Mexico, Canada or any country that has normal relations with Cuba and then taking a direct flight to Havana; or, legally, by traveling via a U.S. sanctioned "people-to-people" program. We chose Friendly Planet's *Colors of Cuba* for our tour.

In nine days, our "people-to-people" experience gave us a snapshot of Cuba today. We visited a medical clinic, organic farm, senior citizen home, school, national park, Che Guevara's memorial, and the cities of Havana, Cienfuegos, and Trinidad. We also explored Ernest Hemingway's home, a synagogue and had some unexpected surprises along the way.

Entering old Havana felt like a dream. *This can't be real.* We were greeted by mildew covered old colonial style buildings everywhere that hadn't been touched, cleaned or repaired in a half a century. Balconies with rusted wrought iron rails, cracks in virtually every structure, rotted wooden shutters, and clothes hanging to dry from windows and doorways were pervasive. It felt like a scene from an old Mad Max movie, in which the civilized world had come to an end, leaving pockets of people to scramble, to make do with what they had.

And "make do" is exactly what the Cubans have been doing, starting with the old American cars left behind when relations between the U.S. and Cuba came to a screeching halt. Plymouths, DeSotos, Chevy Bel Airs, Studebakers, Packards from the 1950's are everywhere. Some are used as taxis, others for personal transportation.

Our Cuban tour guide, Norberto, met us at Havana's International airport. The airport was, as all things are in Cuba, a throwback to the 1950's. Its sparsely decorated interior and low voltage fluorescent lighting said, in so many words, "Bienvenidos a Cuba," the land that time forgot.

In his early forties, with short black hair and wearing an over-washed, over-worn, reddish-orange polo shirt, a shirt that would be his trademark for the next nine days, Norberto ushered us toward our bus for an initial tour of Havana. Nor, as we called him, spoke perfect English, had a couple of college degrees and most importantly possessed a sense of humor, which would come in handy as we negotiated our way through Cuban culture in the following days.

In Havana, we dropped by an elementary school, and an artist's production studio, saw centuries-old fortresses and ate at government run restaurants for lunch and dinner. Cuban food in the U.S. has developed a reputation as a flavorful fusion of Spanish, African and Caribbean cuisines. So it was a bit of shock to find out that Cuban food in Cuba is anything but flavorful. It's on the bland side. A typical meal might be chicken and rice with a green vegetable. Norberto explained that hotels and restaurants were owned by the government which helped to explain the lack of imaginative dishes available. We would though, in the coming days, be treated to some Paladars, privately owned restaurants, which serve a variety of flavorful dishes.

Havana, with a population of two and a half million people is actually two cities – the old city or "old Havana," with its original colonial architecture, and the suburbs where newer structures are located. In spite of the deteriorating physical state of old Havana, UNESCO deemed it as a World Heritage site in 1982 because of its colonial architecture and historic fortifications. In the suburbs we saw the influence of the former Soviet Union, with ugly concrete-grey public housing buildings everywhere; stark, without balconies, blackened with mildew stains and of course, laundry hanging from windows and doorways. Welcome to Cuba.

When Christopher Columbus landed in Cuba he wrote "this land is the most beautiful that the human eye has ever seen." The ride from Havana to the cities of Trinidad and Cienfuegos, five hours south, introduced us to Columbus' view of Cuba – with a patchwork of lush green valleys, rising up in the distance to form small mountains. Good roads, little traffic, it was all so peaceful and serene on the way to Trinidad; hard to imagine an area so picturesque was, not so long ago, caught up in an insurrection that would determine Cuba's fate for the next half century.

Trinidad, a town in the province of Sancti Spíritus, is located on the coast in the central part of Cuba. It's a well-preserved community boasting a population of 100,000. Our four-star hotel, a joint venture between Spain and Cuba, sat in the town center, on the plaza, great for people watching when time allowed.

Trinidad's main industry is tobacco processing, but originally, sugar cane gave the town its reason for being. Today, tourism is bringing in a much needed economic infusion, with pristine white sand beaches and inviting turquoise water only a few minutes from town.

The politics of Cuba gives new meaning to the word contradiction. On one hand, everyone has food, with the help of their ration card, and everyone has a free education and free health care. On the other hand, it is not uncommon for doctors who are paid less than $200 a month to drive taxi cabs to supplement their income. In fact, most Cubans supplement their incomes in order to survive, according to Nor. On one hand the world cheered - including the U.S. - as the romantic charismatic Fidel toppled the tyrant Juan Batista. On the other hand, millions of Cubans have fled due to the brutal repression of the Castro regime. Fidel, who had frustrated, but outlasted nine American presidents, has put his political mark on this island country of 11 million.

On our government approved tour, the Cubans we saw seemed to be okay with their lot in life, enjoying music and sports, and they apparently have live bands wherever they go. On a trip to a national park, we pulled up at 11:00 a.m. and were treated to Mojitos and a live salsa band. After twenty minutes or so, another tourist bus pulled up, free Mojitos and free band. No Cubans in old DeSotos pulled up for their free breakfast cocktail. Workers' paradise? Or, an attempt by the Cuban government to project an unrealistic view of Cuban life?

Back in Havana for the remaining days of our Cuban adventure, we went to a "pairing" event. In the U.S., pairing is normally associated with a certain food paired with a certain wine. But in this case it was a pairing of Cuban coffee, Cuban rum and a Cuban cigar. And of course, there was a salsa band. The event turned out to be great fun, even though I'm sure that most of our group, if not all, were not cigar smokers. They all gave it a few puffs, took a lot of photos and laughed a lot.

That evening, it was off to salsa dance lessons and a farewell dinner party. The restaurant was a Paladar, so the food was plentiful and tasty.

As we boarded the bus for our trip to the airport, Nor answered the few remaining questions that people may have had. Everyone in our group had a sense that Cuba is changing. Nor confirmed our suspicions, stating, "You're lucky to see Cuba now, at the beginning of this great change." He went on to explain how the trade embargo was hindering Cuba's development, but Cuba would move forward in spite of these restrictions.

With a nation dependent on food rationing, free education and free medical services, this change will have to be well managed, because Cuba is worn thin, teetering between the promises of revolutionary rhetoric and the somber need for a higher standard of living.

Heading through security, I turned around for one last glimpse at this fascinating country, and there was Nor, big smile, waving – wearing that same over-washed, over-worn, reddish-orange shirt.

# Golda, May You Someday Rest in Peace

*By Morris Crisci*

## A One Act Play

*S**OLOMON** Katz is seated on a park bench waiting for his friend Abraham Leibowitz to join him for their afternoon chat.*

**ABE:** *(Entering somewhat downcast)* Solly my friend, how goes the battle?

**SOL:** Abe you're late. I was beginning to wonder if you were coming at all.

**ABE:** Would I ever miss our afternoons together? It was Golda, may she rest in peace, who would say, "That Solomon Katz is a good man and a good friend. Stay close to him. He is good medicine for you."

**SOL:** So, tell this good man and good friend why you're so late.

**ABE:** Eh … Bank business … it took longer than expected. *(shaking his head in disgust)* Those vultures picking at your bones for whatever flesh you have left!

**SOL:** Sit down my friend. Talk to me. And here, have some dates. They're good for you.

**ABE:** *(Pausing and looking at Sol)* I can't.

**SOL:** You can't? Why not?

**ABE:** Look where you're sitting.

**SOL:** Abe we've been sitting here for forty-five years! What are you talking about?

**ABE:** *(Patiently and deliberately)* Solly, take a good look at where you are sitting.

**SOL:** What? Is the paint wet? Did I sit on some pigeon poop? What?

**ABE:** You're sitting on my side.

**SOL:** *(Sarcastically)* Ah, of course! How stupid of me! What possessed me to be so presumptuous and insensitive to my best friend? Sitting on **his** side of the bench! Please forgive me.

**ABE:** *(Thinking Sol was sincere)* O, Solly, I know you didn't mean to…

**SOL:** *(Interrupting)* Abe, are you crazy? What difference does it make what side of this bench you sit on?

**ABE:** *(Trying to reason with Sol)* Where is it that my Golda and I would **always** sit?

**SOL:** I never really paid much attention to that. You were always here before us. My Sarah and I would just sit where you and Golda were not. That's all!

**ABE:** So, is that it? Just because I'm a little late you take it upon yourself to commandeer my side of the bench? *(Wringing his hands)* What would Golda say, may she rest in peace?

**SOL:** Golda would say you're nuts! Now sit down and stop being such a foolish old man!

**ABE:** I can't! I just can't! It wouldn't feel right! Golda wouldn't approve!

---

**SOL:** Abe, my good friend, Golda has been gone for over two years, for goodness sake. It's always "Golda this" or "Golda that." I haven't said this before, but, you've got to let her go.

**ABE**: It's been two years, one month and three days. How can I let go of someone who meant everything to me? All I have left are my memories.

**SOL:** *(Pleading)* Abe, stop it! Don't you see what you are doing to yourself? *(Pause; getting no reaction, he goes on)* You know how much I loved my Sarah, right? *(Turning away from Abe, facing the audience)* She was the reason I lived. I didn't need the sun or the moon or the fresh air. There was Sarah.

*(Slight pause; standing and moving toward the audience, forgetting for a moment where he was)*

God did not see fit to bless us with children. But that did not matter. I had my beloved Sarah. She was more than anyone could ever hope for. I would look at her in the kitchen making one of her sumptuous creations. Seeing her would make me forget the glorious aroma of her cooking. And when I watched her working in her flower garden it was like the blossoms were straining to look as beautiful as her. My God, when she touched me, it was like the world stopped and was put on hold. And when I heard her voice it was like the song of an angel … bringing comfort to my ears and joy to my soul.

*(Holding his pose for a moment; then returning to reality from savoring his thoughts. Soberly, turning back to Abe)*

You see, my loss was great too, Abe. It wasn't too long after you lost Golda. I miss Sarah, just like you miss Golda. It hurts me, just like it hurts you. *(Resting a hand Abe's shoulder)* But, we have to move on. You have to let her go just like I let go of my Sarah. *(Pause, pleading)* Abe, let Golda rest in peace.

**ABE:** *(After a long pause to let this sink in, turning to Sol)* I'm so sorry my friend. I had no idea you hurt so much. *(With resolve)* I will try, Solly. I will. I promise.

**SOL:** Good! Now let's sit down. *(Starting to sit on "Abe's side" he stops and motions to Abe yielding this side of the bench)* After you. *(They both give a chuckle)*

**ABE:** *(Removing his coat and draping it over the seat back he sits as does Sol)* Solly, I'll have one of those dates now.

**SOL:** *(As he hands over the bag of dates)* Something was troubling you. You didn't paint such a good picture of the people at the bank. What did they do to you?

**ABE:** Ah, you don't want to know.

**SOL:** Why would I ask you if I didn't want to know?

**ABE:** It's one of those private matters. I don't think I can talk to you about it. Golda always said … I mean I have been told that there are matters that can only be discussed within the family.

**SOL:** So, I suppose you can talk to your sons who are located who-knows-where on the other side of the world. Is that it?

**ABE:** Oh no! Golda … what I meant to say is we should never trouble the kids with our problems. They have their own to deal with.

**SOL:** Okay, let me see if I've got this straight. Golda is gone. Your boys are away and you wouldn't be able to talk with them even if they were here. Right?

**ABE:** Yes, that's right.

**SOL:** So, what about me? Am I chopped liver?

**ABE:** Oh no Solly, you're my best friend. But, you're not family.

**SOL:** Abe, I'm the closest thing to family you have left. Trust me. *(Pause)* Remember what Golda said, may she rest in peace, "That Solomon Katz is a good man and a good friend." Remember?

**ABE:** Yes, but… I'm so ashamed.

**SOL:** Ashamed? What could my best friend Abraham Leibowitz be so ashamed of? What did you do?

**ABE:** It's not what I've done. It's what I didn't do!

**SOL:** So … what didn't you do?

**ABE:** *(Shaking his bowed head says nothing)*

**SOL:** *(Gently coaxing)* Abe, I'm not the FBI. Talk to me.

**ABE:** *(Pausing and barely able to say)* They're taking my house.

**SOL:** Taking your house? How can this be?

**ABE:** Golda's medical bills … final expenses … I haven't been able to recover … I just got further and further behind … I'm so ashamed … I'm so lousy with money … not like Golda … that's for sure.

**SOL:** *(Thinking for a moment)* Abe, this isn't the end of the world. We can work this out … together.

**ABE:** Golda would be so ashamed of me… "My husband the street person!" *(Pause)* Sol, you know how much I like this bench? I would hate that it should be my bed from now on!

---

**SOL:** Stop it! You're not going to be a street person, sleeping on this or any other bench. *(Pause)* Worst case, you come stay with me.

**ABE:** *(Amazed)* Solly, you would do that for me? Why would you do such a thing?

**SOL:** Why not. My house is paid for. I've got plenty of room. My expenses are not that great. And, you don't look like you eat that much. *(Pause)* Besides, I can use the company.

**ABE:** Golda was right about you! You are a good man and a good friend.

**SOL:** Then it's settled. We'll see what we can still do about your house. If it's too late, you will have a new home with me. A deal? *(Extends hand to Abe)*

**ABE:** A deal…on one condition.

**SOL:** Okay, what condition?

**ABE:** I must pay my share of the expenses.

**SOL:** Oh Abe**,** let's not worry about that right now. We'll deal with that later.

**ABE:** No, we have to agree now! Golda would have it no other way. She says we must always carry our own weight.

**SOL:** Okay Abe! Okay! You can carry your own weight!

**ABE:** *(Pacified)* Thank you! Thank you, my friend! *(Shakes his hand … turns to retrieve his coat)*

**SOL:** *(Shaking his head, turning away from Abe, looking toward heaven, uttering under his breath)* Golda, may you **someday** rest in peace.

*(Lights fade to black as the two remain in their final poses)*

# Silence

*By Rebecca Johnson*

A taste of a love brushed whisper

Wisps of feathers in a breeze

Footsteps on sand

A far away memory calling back

A drizzle in a long ago dream

Losing a song

Breathing out dim moments

Standing in the velvet glow at dusk

A shadow of the lost and forgotten

# Hibou The Owl

*By Robert McLoughlin* ———————————

Above the tree tops high aloft
You soar on wings of velvet soft

Your golden eyes so round and wide
Find tiny creatures where they hide

With talons cruel and piercing beak
You slay them as they squirm and shriek

When I question who are you
You answer Hibou that's hoo
Hoo-hoo-hoo
Hooo-hooo

# F243

*By K. J. Baird*

S O it begins. That feeling of losing one's humanity, of becoming just another faceless number in the crowd, and all I've done is turn into the parking lot. "Oh YES," I say as I snag a coveted parking spot, hoping it's a good omen. I watch other cars circling the asphalt like hungry vultures and tell myself it won't be that bad. It can't possibly take the entire afternoon. After all, I have an appointment, and all I'm doing is getting a new driver's license and registration. It's not as if I'm applying for a job or asking to borrow money.

My optimism dims as I gasp at the dismal line snaking out the door, slithering down the sidewalk. Maybe I should see if there is a separate appointment line. Sweet. There is. I queue up and eventually make my way into the building. Do they hold a contest to determine who can come up with the dreariest design when constructing public buildings? It's hard to distract oneself with tan concrete walls and gray industrial tile. Would it really be so tough to apply some color, add a bit of life?

Undaunted, I put on my best smile and greet the woman behind the Plexiglas window. At least as much of a greeting as one can convey through two inches of plastic. Met in return with a blank stare, I am instructed to hand over my documents. In a voice too low for human ears, let alone a crowded waiting room, she instructs me to fill out the forms and get back in line. I'm dismissed before I can say, "Please speak up."

No big deal. I'm a college graduate. How tough can the forms be? Are you kidding me? They want the exact date I purchased my car. Man, it's a 1990. I'm lucky I can remember the year let alone the month and day. I try to recall what the weather was like for a clue to the time of year. It was gray and foggy. Oh wait, I was living in San Francisco. It's always gray and foggy. I'm forced to guess, what are they going to do, throw me in jail? Actually, as I sign under "penalty of law," that is exactly what they say they will do.

I smile as my bored mind plays out a tough prison cell scenario. A lifer approaches me, cigarette dangling from her lips and barks: "Whatcha in for?"

I answer back in a steely, prison-weary voice "I lied about the date I purchased my 23-year-old car."

"Tough crime, tough time," she retorts.

At least I'm momentarily amused as I make my way into the next room. More concrete walls, metal folding chairs and lifeless tile. Wouldn't want it to look inviting or make the masses comfortable – we might not leave. The odor of frustration and fear hangs in the air as I wait for the mechanical voice to call out my number.

Finally! Once again, I try to summon a cheery smile as I step up to the row of Plexiglas windows. No go. I've signed the form per verbal instructions not reading the "do not sign" printed instruction. I scribble my name as the DMV worker glares, looking right through me. I answer her questions, complimenting her on her tennis bracelet. Still no signs of life. It's like talking to a glacier.

Then it happens. Just as I'm about to give up, humanity breaks through. When I'm asked for the official date I brought my car into California I stare blankly. The answer is not simple. She asks the date I started paying rent. I admit quietly and with some embarrassment that I am bartering for my rent. You see, I am an unemployed priest. Laughingly, I share that when I took my vow of poverty, I thought it was metaphorical, not literal. In that moment, amidst my embarrassment and vulnerability, a connection is made and we become real to one another. I am no longer just F243, and she, no longer a lifeless extension of the institution. With genuine warmth and humor, Shirley finishes her portion of the process and wishes me a heartfelt, "Good luck."

It will be another hour and a half before I leave, temporary license in hand. In the end, it isn't as bad as I'd feared. It has taken all afternoon. But even in the cattle call of waiting patrons, and the bleakness of industrial strength decor, humanity lives, if only for a moment. But sometimes, a moment is all it takes.

# John F. Kennedy... shot

*By Norma Kipp Avendano*

FRIDAY, November 22, it was almost a week until Thanksgiving. Sitting in the teachers' lounge, I was thinking of the sculptured paper turkeys my students would make in the art lesson when recess ended. The bell to summon all to classrooms had not yet rung, but I rose to go. At the door, I met the principal, white-faced and solemn, who had shocking, unbelievable news. She said, "A radio bulletin says President Kennedy has just been shot in Dallas. He's been rushed to Parkland Hospital. It sounds bad. Don't say anything yet to your students, but be prepared to tell them something by lunch time. By then there should be… good…or bad…news. I'll send a monitor around as soon as I hear something more."

Teachers, mute with shock of this unthinkable occurrence, left to collect their children and escort them to their classrooms. Inside Room 10, I distributed art materials to my fourth grade students and demonstrated the making of a sample turkey, then sank into my chair at my desk. A position unusual for me since I always circulated among the students as they worked, giving help where needed.

Minutes dragged by. My attention was on the window looking out to the flagpole, the lunch tables, and beyond to the door of the principal's office. The clock hands seemed to be standing still as my thoughts raced … waiting … hoping … praying. One completed fowl was brought to me for pinning to the bulletin board, then another. I was pinning a third when the door opened and an office monitor entered, carrying a message mounted on black paper. I reached for it, read it, checked my name off the routing list, and returned it to the pale-faced messenger.

I walked slowly to my desk, and leaned against it. "Class..." I began, hardly recognizing my own voice. The children looked up, waiting. I began again, "Class, I have some very sad news. President Kennedy has been shot. You know he went to Dallas today. That's where it happened. He was taken to a hospital, but it was too late. He has died."

The children sat like frozen statues, scissors poised, paste on fingers, crayons pressed to paper. Then, as one, their eyes turned to the window where the patrol boys were slowly lowering the drooping flag to half-mast; one was playing taps, rather badly. As the last note died, the noon bell rang.

Over the next few days, it was if the entire nation stopped to watch the movement passing across television screens: the succession of Lyndon Baines Johnson to the office of the President of the United States; eulogies for the slain president; comparison of the two fallen Presidents Kennedy and Lincoln, ninety-eight years apart; preparations for the great state funeral; the procession of the white horses bearing the coffin to the rotunda followed by the rider-less horse; the muffled drum beats; and the first family where Mrs. Kennedy and Caroline kissed the flag-draped casket, and young John-John gave his little salute. Finally the burial at Arlington National Cemetery and the lighting of the eternal flame. It was over, and the grieving citizens returned to their daily tasks.

I had admired Mrs. Kennedy from the beginning of her public life, even looking upon her with some small envy as the woman who had it all: poise and breeding, stunning beauty, two precious children, and whose husband was the president of our country. But I envied her no more. In a matter of seconds a bullet had taken her husband, and Jackie was a widow. Even though his life was under attack from cancer, Harry was alive and sitting beside me, returning the pressure of my hand as we witnessed this shattering turn of fate. **President Kennedy dead.** Who could have imagined it a week ago?

# Journey-of-Life

*By Nui Rehfuss*

EVERY living creature is born for a reason. Here is what we know. Life may take us on many different paths to explore and experience, discover and learn along the way. If we have trust, focus and confidence in ourselves, there are many opportunities in every direction. We have to answer difficult questions, rise to challenges and adapt ourselves to any adventure on the journey. Lao Tzu said, "Do the difficult things while they are easy and do the great things while they are small. A journey of a thousand miles begins with a single step."

2014 is here. We are looking forward to embracing the next 365 days of journey. Each day, each week and each month will be different and will be filled with unpredictable unknowns. Shall we trust something that we cannot see? Yes! The journey of our lives combines many factors, but the three simplest are:

1.      It is not about getting there – it is a learning process.
2.      It is not about how quickly one can arrive, but it is to understand and deliver the important message on time.
3.      It is not about achieving our goal, but what we take away from our experience and our own self-fulfillment.

\* \* \*

Our lives are our journey. The process of getting there is to develop our skills by beginning with positive thinking, knowing our strengths, determining our expectations, accepting our actions and having the courage to continue on the journey. On the way we will meet and touch many lives. Sometimes we connect and learn from them. Sometimes we just observe and appreciate them. And sometimes, we teach them. Disruptions or distractions on the expedition make our lives more interesting, and at the end, may help to guide us.

To understand the beauty of life, time plays a major role. Heartache and discomfort occur everywhere on the paths. These may cause us to drop some current projects. When we see something new, bright and shiny, it grabs our attention. Everything is high priority on the journey. We must take charge and take on our responsibilities, with self-discipline and plan to complete our project on time. It is a new day every 24 hours. If some problem shows up on our way, we should evaluate, understand and solve the problem before moving onto our next priority.

Success, or achieving our goal, is a state of mind. We define success or achievement to different levels depending on individual goals. It has no single definition to many people. On the route of our journey, we may travel through or be trained, and may even become an expert in some specialty, which makes us what we are today. To feel our joy and our freedom on this planet means a lot to every living life.

In the process of being alive and being healthy, we never stop learning or improving ourselves. Those two things have no limit. For sure, no one can take away our personal knowledge, personal growth, personal experience, or personal precious moments. We must continue our journey in spite of disappointment, discomfort and misfortune along the way. But it is most important that we allow ourselves to consider, and to challenge as new things arise, testing our courage and doing what is right to benefit all mankind.

# Haircut

*By Rita Early*

"LET them live," my husband whines. He thinks I'm being cruel for trimming the excess vines on my bushy tomato plant.

"I'm not growing this plant for decorative reasons," I explain. Snip. "In order for it to produce good fruit the suckers must die." Snip-snip. "See this vine without any flowers?"

"Yeah."

"It's a sucker. I read on the internet that the vine will extract water and nutrients but produce no fruit, resulting in fewer tomatoes on the fruit-bearing vines. Don't worry. I won't get rid of all of them. The plant needs the leaves for photosynthesis." Snip-snip, snip. "The trick is not to cut too many." Snip, snip-snip.

"How do you know when it's too many?"

I look over the plant, now half bald, and nod with certainty.

"When it dies." Snip, snip-snip. Snip.

# The Replacement

*By Frank Primiano*

I dislike driving in the dark, especially in unfamiliar territory. Animals and other obstacles always jump out at me, or at least that's what I imagine.

My problem tonight is that a non-imaginary obstacle just flattened my right rear tire. I'm stopped, here in the middle of nowhere, on the side of a dirt road bordered by overgrown weeds and drooping trees. And what's that up there? In my headlights? A driveway almost hidden by shrubs? And a gate under a large arch? With letters formed into the metalwork? What do they say? "Cemetery?" Oh, shit. That's all I need.

Triple-A can fix my tire, but where am I? Maybe if I get the name of the cemetery they might find me.

I have to leave the car for a closer look. This place seems deserted, and I'll be right up ahead. So it should be safe enough to leave the engine running for my headlights ... don't want to lose my battery, too.

Just in case, I'll take my flashlight. Where is it? Ah, right where it should be, in the glove compartment.

Here goes.

Gravel on the driveway crunches as I walk to the gate. A chilly breeze rustles the leaves that have fallen, as well as those few still clinging to their branches. The headlights reach a metal plaque imbedded in the stone column supporting the right side of the arch. Everything beyond is in darkness. There's no moon, and the stars are little help.

The number "731" has been cast on the plaque. That's probably the street number, but I still don't know the street's name. Or the cemetery's.

The gate's open. My flashlight penetrates the shadows beyond. I see grey shapes – some upright, some leaning at angles, others lying flat – amid a bumper crop of weeds. And what's that? Inside the fence? A bicycle. Maybe I can use it. I have to go through the gate to get a better look.

I'm in the cemetery now. The stillness, not the cold, makes me shiver.

The bike's in good shape, not old and rusty. Judging from the way it's resting on top of the grass, it can't have been parked here very long ago, maybe even today. Damn. It's chained to the fence. I sigh, realizing I'll never be able to open the lock.

My disappointment yields to confusion. Why's it here? Is its rider still around? In the dark? That's a disturbing thought.

I hear rustling close behind me. I turn my head and see a writhing, white apparition coming at me along the ground from out of the darkness. I jump a foot backwards, almost falling. It encircles my legs. My heart races, pounding in my ears. I barely maintain control of my vocal chords and my bladder. I kick violently to get it off me before I realize it's just a newspaper page-sized sheet of white paper.

The breath that I'd been holding escapes my lips. I bend over, gasping, grab the paper, and hold it up. One side is blank. The other has the full-scale image of a tombstone with its inscriptions. Someone must've been doing rubbings and this one got away.

My heart tries to settle down. I swing my light. More sheets of paper flutter along the ground. Some snag at the bases of trees; others hang up on sprawling bushes. Each has the likeness of a headstone engraving on it. Were these discarded or accidentally dropped? In either case, a lot of work's been wasted.

I point the light into the distant blackness ahead. I see no movement other than swaying weeds and branches and their shadows. Is the rubbings person still nearby?

I martial my courage and say, "Hello," in a quavering voice only slightly louder than normal. No response.

I fake bravery and shout, "Is anybody here?" Again, no answer. I wait.

I should get the heck out of this place and try to fix that flat myself. Screw the auto club. It'll take them forever to get here even after they figure out where I am.

As I turn to retrace my steps to the gate, the beam of light finds another sheet of paper. It covers a horizontal gravestone installed flush with the ground like a slab in a sidewalk. The grave is on the other side of the path, two rows from where I stand. The paper flaps in the wind, but it remains in place. That's odd, very odd.

I take one tentative step, then another, following my flashlight's lead. I reach the grave site. All is quiet except for the occasional rustling of dried vegetation and what sounds like the hoot of an owl or, perhaps, the moan of a distant dog. I glance from side to side and then behind me. I tell myself I'm not scared, only that I want no more surprises.

The paper covering the gravestone at my feet is anchored at the upper end by a row of rocks along its edge. That's why it hasn't blown away. The image of only half the inscription on the stone has been transferred to the paper: "William James Lacey, January 3, 1792 – February 18, 1857,

Lived a Good" is all that is there. It's as though the person doing the rubbings were interrupted in the middle of the job.

I look at nearby sites. Nothing seems out of place until my beacon catches a swatch of color. It's just beyond the top edge of the grave. I take two steps and stand over it. A piece of faded cloth protrudes from the ground at the head of the tombstone. I bend to pick it up but the soil maintains its grip. Dropping to my knees, I prop the flashlight so that it shines on the spot. I push chunks of earth aside. It's loose, as though it'd been dug up and replaced recently. There are bony footprints in the soil. Someone's been trying to tamp it flat. That's odd, very odd.

Using two hands, I scoop up more dirt. The cloth is freed. I hold it in the light. It's a torn, tie-dyed T-shirt reminiscent of the time when hippies roamed the earth. The fabric hangs in shreds from my hands. The realization hits me that it must have been decaying for some time. I drop it, not wanting to touch it any longer.

The fragment falls, drawing my attention to the depression in the ground from which it had come. Something glints. I root in the dirt with one hand and touch a cold, hard object, a hunk of metal. Lifting it, I find it's attached to a short leather strap. The metal object is a corroded belt buckle with the engraved figure of a naked woman still visible on it. The piece of disintegrating belt attached to it is about two inches wide, in the style of the 1960's and 70's.

This arouses my interest. What else is buried here? I begin removing handfuls of dirt, careful not to miss any possible treasure, perhaps a wallet, or a watch, or some coins. In about 15 minutes I've pulled out the rest of the loose soil. All I find is a large, black, wax crayon; hardly worth the effort. I'm left with a semicircular hole as wide as the gravestone and several feet deep.

I shine the light into the pit. A vertical piece of dirt-encrusted wood has been exposed. I assume that this board is the end of Mr. William James Lacey's coffin. Lying on my belly, I reach into the hole and run my hand over the wood. I'm not sure what kind of tree it came from or how it was treated, but it seems pretty sturdy given its age from the inscription on the tombstone.

Oh, God. Under my touch, it moves a little. It's loose. I hook the fingers of my right hand on the top of the board and pull. It swings down exposing the contents of the box. I ignore the rest of the world, not at all as scared as I should be.

The first thing that strikes me is a smell. Not the overpowering stench of rotting bones and moldy wood and clothes. No, the faint scent of a perfume wafts from the old casket. That's odd, very odd.

More curious than ever, I shine my light into the black cavity. I see hair, reddish-brown hair. Not the scraggly strands I'd expect on a decayed corpse. No, it's a full head of disheveled, medium length hair that surrounds a face, not a skull. From my position above, the face looks like that of a woman who, if she is dead, hasn't died very long ago.

I reach both hands inside the box, grab the woman's jacket and pull as hard as I can. She slides out until her head and shoulders are exposed in the hole that I've just dug. I wipe my hands on my coat and put my fingers to her neck to check for a pulse the way I've seen in the movies. I've never done this before, so I'm not sure how conclusive my findings will be. Nevertheless, no matter how I try, I find none.

Shining the light on her neck, I see bruising and smudges of dirt. Several individual marks stand out. Could they have been made by fingers?

While I consider what to do next, the world that I've been ignoring imposes itself upon me. Still on my belly, the upper half of my body lying in the hole, I hear the revving of an engine. I arch my back and lift my head to look toward the road that's just beyond the fence, perhaps thirty feet away. There's my car. Its lights are still on, but someone's behind the wheel.

The car begins to move. I can't make out the driver's face in the dark. The glow of the dashboard instruments reflects off a pale, gaunt head, and cadaverous, white shoulders and chest. Bony, fleshless fingers grasp the steering wheel.

The car picks up speed. I hear the flapping of the flat tire as it is forced to roll. My hands slip in the soft dirt when I try to rise to protest this outrage. I am unaware of the arms reaching up from the hole until their hands have me tightly around my neck.

\* \* \*

I know my eyes are open, but I see only black. I'm flat on my back. No stars are visible. All is silent. I hear nothing, not even the beating of my heart.

I try to get up but hit my head on something after raising it only a few inches. The bump makes a hollow sound that echoes around me. I move my hands and feet. They also contact obstacles.

Where am I? God, not in the coffin? I can't be. I don't handle confined spaces well. And I'll run out of air. I'll suffocate.

But it's odd, very odd. I'm not panicked the way I know I should be. And I don't feel the need to breathe. I'm calm ... because I know someone will find me ... eventually. After all, I found that woman on her first day. Of course, the guy before her must have been lying here for decades. And who knows how long William James Lacey took to snag someone?

Any day, somebody'll find my half-buried flashlight and start digging. It's gonna happen. It's only a matter of time. All I have to do is wait ... and be ready.

# Compost

*By Jean E. Taddonio*

Words and ideas

stew 'round my brain

like scraps of fertile leftovers

in a steamy compost pile

They sift and brew together

formless

like people on a crowded summer's lawn

waiting for a concert

ripe with perfumed sweat

When the music starts, the heap of soil

rich from man's beginnings

and his ends

begins to dance and so do I

Life sprouts once again

A poem is born

# Under New Management

*By Alastair McAulay*

LFRED inherited the Sunshine Diner from his father. A handsome young man in his twenties, Alfred never, in his wildest dreams, wished to be involved in running the place. Growing up, he observed how hard his father worked to make money. In fact, he felt that worries over the diner had contributed to his father's recent heart attack.

The Sunshine looked all of its 100 years, both inside and out. It still served eggs over easy with hash browns for two dollars and chicken pie with mashed potatoes for four dollars. Low wages and the dismal surroundings led to a continual turnover of waitresses. Two years earlier a McDonald's had opened nearby which reduced business at the diner. Then The Greater Tire Company, a major industry in town, filed for bankruptcy.

Because he had not been as successful at selling used medical devices as he had expected to be when he was the star quarterback in high school, Alfred decided to focus on what to do with his new business. He mentioned his inheritance to his many friends. They arranged to meet at the diner for lunch to discuss possibilities for its future.

Their consensus was that, rather than put the diner up for sale, Alfred should try to run it with their help in attracting customers. Henry, whose father owned a construction company, offered to inspect the diner and make remodeling recommendations. Penelope, a branch manager in the Steubenville National Bank, said, "We're a small regional bank. This is just the sort of investment in the local community that we like to support. I'd be pleased to help you prepare a remodeling loan application."

Jeffrey, a large, sporting type, and a connoisseur of local beer, said, "I think you should apply for a liquor license, and I'm willing to work on the necessary documents. Then I can encourage my drinking buddies to hang out here."

George, one of their high school friends, had become a local policeman. "I'm willing to help with security." Mary offered to be a part-time waitress and recruit some of her friends.

Finally they addressed the menu. No one was impressed with it. "It looks like a list of the contents of an overstuffed refrigerator and freezer," Evangelica said. "And your pies … they taste like they're old and have been frozen and then zapped in a microwave. My mother, Frances, and I specialize in baking fruit pies that will make you yearn for more. We could bring some in for a grand opening of the new diner."

"Good idea," said Michelle, Alfred's girlfriend who worked in advertising. "We could publicize the Sunshine's new management in the local paper and announce that those coming to the opening will get a free slice of your delicious pie for dessert."

\*　\*　\*

At the grand opening, Evangelica, true to her word, arrived carrying a stack of twenty boxed pies. A large crowd came, and she had to return to her car to fetch more. To Alfred's surprise there was an equally large crowd the following day and the next. He was amazed that even those customers who didn't normally eat dessert pies were lining up for a slice of pie. There was so much demand that Alfred asked, "Hey, Evie, what's in the pies?"

"Didn't you know? These are pot pies."

Alfred frowned. "Not like the pot pies I'm used to."

"I mean, marijuana pies," Evangelica said.

Alfred put his hand to his head. *Oh, no!* he thought. Then, after further reflection he gave Evangelica a wink and said, "Go on baking the pies, but don't give the recipe to anyone!"

The Sunshine Diner became one of the most popular haunts in town.

# A good intention clothes itself in sudden power*

*By Lindsay Elise Reph*

A few years ago I told my sister-in-law, Rachel, about wanting to start a blog. She lives in Seattle, like most of my husband's family, and encouraged me to put my funny comments and interesting stories in one place, something to both close the gap between us and entertain. The only word that came to mind for a title was "Delight," referring to a favorite Bible verse since childhood: "Delight yourself in the Lord and he will give you the desires of your heart." (Psalm 37:4)

As a teenager, I became a fan of *Saturday Night Live*, where Will Ferrell did a hilarious impression of James Lipton from *Inside the Actor's Studio*. He would say to guests, "You are a delight." Since the word is a thread woven throughout my life, I thought about what delights me in hopes that a title would magically pop into my newly-minted writer brain. Standing with Rachel in the quaint town square of Bloomfield, Iowa, I felt embarrassed to say out loud the only inspiration I'd had. Fraulein Maria from *The Sound of Music* began singing in my head, "Raindrops on roses and whiskers on kittens…" Anyone who knows me well, knows how I love animals, and kitties in particular, so why not call it "Whiskers on Kittens"?

* The title quote is by Ralph Waldo Emerson and inspires me to emerge from my hermit-writer-cave. This blog is powered by a good intention that began years ago.

The answer is: 1. It's cheesy, 2. It's clichéd, and 3. It contains little appeal to people not interested in cats. So I shelved it.

I'd already begun writing about a car accident that nearly took the lives of my younger sister and me in 2002: the year after I graduated with a degree in Psychology and 9/11 blasted a hole straight through the middle of my idealism. My two-week coma and grim prognosis gave way to a recovery that was nothing short of miraculous. But a good writer should show, not tell, so I don't expect you to take my word for it. You'll see ... I hope.

The first ears to hear the early drafts of my story were those of the members in a writer's workshop that meets weekly in Point Loma. Not only were the members kind and encouraging, which I loved, they were also honest and challenging, which I needed. I hoped I could one day call them peers, and early on a few emerged as mentors. The minute I was handed the class syllabus, I knew that I was in the right place, and at the right time. A trusted writer friend from Seattle had just given me an assignment after slogging through my first draft. Her advice was printed on the first line: "You are joining a community of writers..."

Fast forward to a year ago, when inspiration hit again to start blogging, with a renewed energy. I sat on over 60,000 words I'd written about my recovery, told in first person present tense. I'd been on Facebook for only a year, and only because another niece or nephew was about to be born in Seattle. The distance was painful during the unfolding of the birth story, but being in touch with my "in-loves" via Facebook made it less so.

Alas, life's distractions derailed me once more, and though I continued writing and editing my survival story, blogging aspirations fell down mid-flight once again. Through outlets such as the Point Loma Writers Symposium, online conferences, and podcasts, a glaring new issue stared me in the face: I have no platform. I am a writer with a nearly finished book who is virtually nonexistent in the writing world.

Another sister-in-love has a clever, expertly written blog that I have always found delightful. Everything about it is so well done that it became a reason in my mind to hold off on doing my own. For years I've considered Abby a writer, but not myself. Saying the words "I am a writer" caused me to squirm, lower my voice, and watch the face of my listeners to see if they scoffed at the word. No one ever has. I've begun paying attention to this fact.

In the process of learning how to share my story, I became a writer. Perhaps I always was one, but never gave myself credit for preferring essays over multiple choice exams; for being an avid reader who loved writing book reports; or for being a chatterbox who loves to spin a good yarn. It has been an act of intention to define myself in this way.

The survival story is not all that defines me as a writer, but it is the catalyst that brought me to this place. This year, I intend to see this story published. And so with equal parts trepidation and excitement, thus begins my quest.

In the meantime, a place now exists to share my musings, excerpts, successes and failures. The challenge before me is to post weekly, and the most important thing of all: be authentic. And perhaps my story will find publication in the process, whatever that might look like.

I hope you'll join me.

# One Simple Stitch

*By Lindsay Elise Reph*

L AST Thursday, I attended the Point Loma Writers Symposium for the third consecutive year. It usually occurs in late February when the hustle of holiday travels has left behind only warm memories and the newness of spring is bringing forth buds of inspiration.

When I received an email announcing this year's speakers, excitement washed over me. I reserved a seat to hear my favorite nonfiction author, Anne Lamott. I first fell in love with her voice years ago while reading *Bird by Bird*, a book at the top of our recommended reading list for Writer's Workshop. The book contains so much honesty and warmth, alongside writing advice that felt like manna from heaven to this overwhelmed novice.

"You are going to have to give and give and give, or there's no reason for you to be writing. You have to give from the deepest part of yourself, and you are going to have to go on giving, and the giving is going to have to be its own reward. There is no cosmic importance to your getting something published, but there is in learning to be a giver."

For many years, I reveled in seeing words on the page and in clandestine celebrations for small victories. This usually meant finishing a chapter, anywhere from five to fifteen pages, and soaking in the bathtub for hours. A few delights were always part of the revelry: music, scented bath salts, candles, wine. When you go through something like living in hospitals for three months, simplicity of everyday life can be exhilarating.

In the light of the next day, however, I had accomplished very little to the outside world. Responses like, "Oh, are you still writing that?" caused me to doubt myself. Because after all, what was I really doing? Hiding out, writing a story nobody may ever read, and enjoying the thrill that comes from living exactly where one wants to be.

That place was Little Italy, a neighborhood so full of life and beauty that it provided the perfect setting to enjoy my beloved San Diego. Most of my peers were beginning careers, buying homes, making babies. These people do well in the small talk arena, a place I had grown to dread. I had no easy answers to the typical questions, nothing to tie up with a neat little bow until the next social gathering.

And so I grew to love hibernation even more. The writing process did become its own reward.

I received another key piece of advice, this time from a mentor in workshop: try telling the story in a way that lets the reader come along on my journey, revealing only what I knew at the time. As soon as I began this approach, writing became invigorating and took on a life of its own. One of honesty and authenticity. One that provided me with consistent small delights. Each "scene" that stepped out of my memory and onto the page was worthy of celebration.

One nagging question still pestered me: how could I be a giver if I kept the story to myself?

In Anne Lamott's newest book, she says, "If a writer or artist creates from a place of truth and spirit and generosity, then I may be able to enter and ride this person's train back to my own station."

In embracing who I was before the accident and who I have become, I admit that I'm still that sensitive girl whose lip quivers at the thought of an animal suffering, who doesn't respond well to teasing, who finds this world too harsh much of the time. How will that girl toughen up enough to finish a book, publish it, and deal with the inevitable criticism that comes after? Where do I even begin?

In the last chapter of *Stitches*, an answer came, "You find one place in the cloth through which to take one stitch, one simple stitch, nothing fancy, just one that's strong and true. The knot will anchor your thread."

I stood in line waiting to have my book signed with the kind of pure fandom that happens only when you've come into contact with someone you admire who is everything you'd hoped for. I don't remember what I said to her, but I know part of it was "thank you" and what could be more important than that?

After hearing Anne speak, I knew *this* is my stitch. This blog, this place to share, is the stitch I need to move forward. And not just because a title finally came to me, though I have not yet found one for the book.

But I *have* found a knot to anchor my thread.

NOTE: The title quote, cited at length at the end of this post, is from Anne Lamott's book *Stitches: A Handbook on Meaning, Hope, and Repair*. The quote in the middle is from her book *Bird by Bird: Some Instructions on Writing and Life*.

# Damocles' Sword

*By Lloyd Hill*

I still find myself looking in dread at the blinking light.

For ten years I was on red alert every time
there was a message on my answering machine.
Mom, at 90 and a recent widow, had fallen
on the floor unconscious, and her in-home caretaker
had called 911. Mom was in an ambulance
on her way to Kaiser-Zion emergency room.

My sister and I rushed to her side, the doctors
apparently thinking the old lady was dying.
Shirley and I spent the afternoon crying
and saying our last goodbyes over Mom's supine body.

Mom survived that near-death experience
and in subsequent years lived in assisted-living
complexes that better monitored her health but
there were more emergencies and blinking messages
and as she aged, fears of her death heightened.

This year she entered hospice
to help her through her final days.
Shirley and I had more time to cry
and say our last goodbyes.
Mom died September 4, 2013,
just after her 100th birthday.

Still I can't lose the dread of the blinking light.

# Crows

*By Tim Calaway* ―――――――――――――

Thugs of the bird world

Street toughs in black-winged flight suits

Pushing aside the songbirds

That whistle and chirp

Leaving only the Caw Caw laughter

Of the gang of beady-eyed hoods,

Ready to steal anything worth having.

A murder of crows,

A thing devoutly to be wished.*


*Note: No crows were harmed in the writing of this poem.

# A Midsummer Night's Dream

Clouds

Rain

Water

River

Niagara

Viagra

Dole

Pineapple

Hawaii

Fields

Clouds

Rain

Water

Guess I'll have a drink

# Dream Driver

*By Lloyd Hill*

Don't drive anymore awake
but since I quit seven years ago
I drive a lot in my sleep.

Fords, Chevys, Dodges,
I tool around town. Always
crash or lose them though.

Other night cruising a yellow '50
Chevy Coupe, lowered, leaded,
no brakes, I smash into the front
of a restaurant. Last night lost
a silver '67 Lincoln Continental.

Parked on street, went into a bar,
came out drunk, and couldn't find it.
I drink in dreams too. Big ghost
boat wasn't where I thought I left it,

then got into a maroon '49 De Soto
Station Wagon Woody to go
down the road again with Willie
Nelson in my dream where we
drove into a drainage ditch.

So, after driving all night, I
have no desire to get behind
steering wheels awake.

# Sky Dare

*By Jean E. Taddonio*

TODD is the kind of guy who has an expensive hobby. He builds model airplanes. Not the kid kind, but the man kind you fly in – and he flies them: the bi-wing, open cockpit, aerobatic kind. He has come to visit my husband Jim at the Toyota dealership Jim manages. He and Todd used to work together and now see each other less often. I happen to be visiting Jim at the same time.

Todd is showing some photos of his most recent plane. He calls it 'The Spirit Eagle'. Todd is a master pilot and is so good he flies in the pre-flight shows for the Navy's precision flying team, the Blue Angels. He performs stunts.

Jim eagerly invites me to share the photos. "Check this out!" I am duly impressed. Todd's newest creation is painted in rainbows.

"Wow, Todd, this is really beautiful! Do you fly it often?" I say.

"I like to go out on weekends and would like to take my wife up, but she's not buying it."

"Too scared?" I ask. Thinking, *no duh!*

"Yeah I guess."

And then it happens. My Mr. Wonderful, Jim, just has to open his mouth, "Jeane would go up with you."

Todd quickly responds, "Would you?"

"What makes you think I would want to do this?" I respond with a side glare at Jim.

"You have a dare devil streak in you. I bet you'd love it," says Jim.

"Oh yeah? Well, why don't you go!"

"Naw, naw, naw, you're the crazy one, not me." *Really? That's what he thinks? Ah, oh ... I feel the spark of a dare coming on.*

"Well, would you?" Todd is eager.

"Okay, yeah sure, I'll go with you." My words don't convince me of bravery nor do my rolling eyes. But he's serious.

"Okay, great then," he says. "How about next weekend, say Saturday. It will of course depend on the weather. Call me Saturday morning and we'll figure it out." *He is way too excited about this ... it's all moving way too fast. What have I done?* I live and die a thousand times this week.

*Tricks in an acrobatic airplane – he didn't mention tricks – maybe just cruising around?* Truth is, I was afraid to ask. *Why did I say yes? Do I really want to do this? Don't I value my own life? Am I really crazy?* And then I tell myself, *He's an experienced pilot, a professional. He doesn't want to die either.* I tell my kids. That somehow seals the deal. I can't chicken out now. Onward and upward! *Yikes, I'm scared. I'm really scared.*

It's Saturday morning. My heart races before I get out of bed. I slip off my wedding band and my opal ring, giving instructions to Jim about who to give them to if I die. He laughs.

"Oh come on. You'll be fine!" For good measure, I put a barf bag in my jacket along with my Rosary beads and my camera. I've been warned about G-force and how heavy I'll feel as we go up and cold as well. I place the call to Todd and feign matter-of-factness.

"So what do you think? It's a bit hazy out there." A way out perhaps?

"Yeah, it will need to clear up some more for us to go today. Call me after lunch." I'm not sure what to feel now. No lunch for me, that's for sure. I have myself so psyched; every minute of delay is torture. Afternoon comes. I wait awhile to make the call.

He says, "Yeah, I think we're good to go. Come on down. See you in a half hour?"

When I arrive at Gillespie Field, Todd is grinning and ready to go. He has taken his rainbow colored plane out of the hanger and is handing me a set of goggles, a headset and an Amelia Earhart-looking brown leather cap.

"When you want to talk to me or ask questions, all you have to do is press this button, 'cause you know, I'll be sitting right behind you." It is then that I first notice the layout of the two-seater, one behind the other and the passenger seat is up front.

"Are you serious? You mean you are sitting behind me?" By this time I am trying not to go over my own hysteria limit. Ever the consoler, he says, "It'll be fine. You can talk to me anytime. I will keep you 100% informed." *Easy for him to say.* My heart is locked in high gear and ready to give out any minute. I show him my barf bag and my Rosary beads. He laughs while I don my stylish leather cap. He snaps a picture of me and I pray it's not my last. *Okay. It's do or die time. I'm ready. For whatever reason, I have to do this.*

I have always loved to fly, that is, as a passenger in a regular cruise-control big commercial airplane. My trips to see grandkids in Oregon are made even more special by the flights to get there: over the mountains and across the woods, the mystery of clouds looking like islands and the pure miracle of a chunk of metal powered in the sky. Amazing.

Today, however, not sure what to expect, I'm just trying to breathe. We are heading down the runway. My heart is thumping away and voila, we are in the air and at least for now, I am almost good again. It is so weird being up front.

He tunes in, "How you doing so far?"

I answer tentatively, "I'm good ... for now..." We are cruising over the San Diego back country. I am seeing things I've never seen before, like waterfalls, several of them. I test out my talk button.

"I can't believe all the waterfalls!"

"Yeah, huh. We are now over Indian lands. Not too many people get to see what you are seeing. I have special permission from the reservation council to fly over these lands ... pretty."

We fly in silence for about 15 minutes. My heart has dropped from high gear and I am finding myself relaxing. The beauty has won me over. All I've been dreading has gone away. Maybe this is it! Silly me.

But no, not so fast. Todd, the pilot man, speaks again, "So what do you think? We can keep flying like this if you like, or we can do some tricks, entirely your call. We don't have a lot of daylight left though, so let me know."

*Oh damn. Who was I trying to kid. It's decision time for sure, quick before I change my mind.* My words tumble out, "Okay, let's do it. Go for it. That's why I'm here, right?"

"Okay great! Tell you what. I'll describe each trick in detail and you decide which one we'll start with." *He's sounding way too eager. God help me.*

Todd proceeds to detail me his aero "tricks." The first one goes like this: "We go straight up into the sky. You'll feel like you weigh a ton and you'll be real cold. Then we go straight down to where we are looking into the San Diego River bed and for a brief moment I cut the engines while we go upside down and then we are back, right side up again with the engine on!"

I reply, pushing my little talk button, "Yikes! You've got to be kidding! You turn the engine OFF! And we go UPSIDE DOWN!"

"It all happens fast," he says blithely.

*Oh yeah, like that makes it all better*. He then proceeds to outline his other tricks while my heart goes back into high gear. When he's done, all I can say is, "Look Todd, none of them sounds too great to me. How about you do the picking and I'll go along for the ride."

"Okay great. Here's what we'll do. We'll do the first one I described. Remember?"

*Like I could forget that one*. "I remember."

"I won't pull any surprises. I'll tell you everything," he says. *That's reassuring?*

As we climb the sky, I feel a sense of unmistakable awe, like looking straight into the face of blue heaven. My blood is surging and I feel heavy as an anchor. I even try to lift my tiny camera and can barely open the shutter to snap a shot from seat level. Before I know it there is silence.

*Oh my God, oh my God*. The engine is off and I'm looking into the river bed and now I'm upside down ... whoa ... and back side up again and the engine is on! YAHOO! We did it! I'm alive and well and as excited as if I'd climbed Mt Everest! "YAHOO!" I'm pushing the button so he'll hear me: "YAHOO!" He's laughing.

"So you liked it?"

"I loved it!" There, I said it and it's true!

"Great! So you want to do some more?"

"Heck, yeah!" I surprise myself! We proceed to do about four more tricks from spiraling on our side to various forms of loops and spins. I am ecstatic. Amazing grace. We're in the air about 90 minutes altogether, and Todd lands his bright beauty like the pro he is.

Feet on the ground, my legs and my belly feel wobbly. I announce, "Now I think I'm going to be sick."

Todd quick to assure me, "No, no you're good. You did great! Just keep walking and I'll get you a Coke." I feel like I'm still flying high. Look out, world! There's nothing I can't do! ... except maybe bungee jump. Now that's scary!

# Snuffy

*By David S. Larson*

I sit in the far back seat of our tan Ford station wagon and look at the disappearing suburban street. Snuffy, our cocker spaniel, becomes smaller with each rotation of our whitewall tires.

He stares at me confused, and then turns to sniff something on the ground which attracts his nose.

Tears come down my face and I don't know why. All Snuffy ever did was bark and nip at me. My father finally turns a corner and I know Snuffy is gone forever. A loss from somewhere deep inside my five year-old body brings on sobs. "It's okay. He'll find a good home," my father assures.

The rest of the car is silent. Dan and Steve, my two older brothers say nothing, my mother stoic, as always, in the front seat holding my baby sister Kris. Finally, "David. Come on now. Big boys don't cry," she snorts.

Our car is packed as much as humanly possible. The roof sags under the burden of old suitcases filled with must-have clothes and small treasures – things we didn't allow the Italian movers to touch. Yet, we've left so much behind.

All my mind pictures is that last look Snuffy gave me. I suppose my father saw him too through his side view mirrors. But he's the one who said we had to let him go, so how he feels doesn't matter.

We pull onto the highway. There are no signs in Minnesota which say "Pasadena" on them, a place I've only heard about but don't understand. The longest trip I'd ever taken is during summers to visit my grandparents at Lake Blanche – just one of the 10,000 dotted across our state.

After half an hour, my father pulls off the road. "Paul, why are we stopping?" my mother asks.

I turn to see him nod out the window and she just shrugs.

We're in front of a Foster's Freeze. "Who wants an ice cream?" my father says.

I wipe my tears and climb over the seat, my brothers already exited and running to the window.

"Paul, don't dip mine," my mother shouts after him.

My father takes my hand. I don't care about being a big boy now. I just want to feel safe and know I'm loved. And know I'll never be left behind. "He'll be fine. And so will we, David," my father says.

We order. I sit with my father and brothers on a faded green bench outside in the bright sun. There's an art to eating a Foster's Freeze on a hot summer day when you've abandoned your dog.

No matter how fast I turn the cone and my little tongue laps up the mess, it still finds a way to get onto my hands and drip in small white tears onto my blue shirt. My father just smiles at me and I smile back.

Licking my fingers will be the best part of my day.

# The Comics

*By Mary Carnes*

---

MY husband and I like getting the paper delivered to our driveway in the early hours of the day. Whoever is up first puts on the coffee, collects the paper and brings it to the bedroom. When the bed is made, we settle in with our morning pick-me-up and grab a piece of the news.

For a time, paying for the *San Diego Union-Tribune* fell to me until I cancelled my subscription after an unexpected rate increase. Then, when the paper called, as they always do when you cancel, my husband, Ranse, talked with them and got a reduced price. Later, he, too, got fed up when they again raised their rate and ordered the *Los Angeles Times* instead. This costs him about $2 a week. He really prefers getting the *San Diego UT*, and he prefers their comics, too.

But this story isn't about different newspapers and it isn't about me, either. It's about my husband, Ranse. He really likes the comics. After Sports, it's the next thing he looks at. If we are reading in bed, he'll turn to me and hand me the funnies.

"Here, read *B.C.*" – or *Crankshaft*, or *The Fusco Brothers*, or something else. "It's really good."

Most of the time I don't think it's as humorous as he does. But, once in awhile, I agree with his perception of a particular strip and chuckle before handing the paper back. "Yeah, that is good."

One of his favorite comic strips is *Mary Worth*. Mary must be about 100 years old by now, but she is slimmer than ever, very modern looking, and quite gorgeous for a white-haired, older lady. She even has a boyfriend, and she still travels all over the place. Mary is quite the philosopher. Ranse gets a big kick out of her because she loves to help people and usually gives counsel that is such "fluff" it makes one's eyes roll.

But, the *Los Angeles Times* does not carry *Mary Worth,* and when we don't get the *Union Tribune,* Ranse has to look for his beloved "Mary" on the Internet so he doesn't miss a single day of her guidance.

Another comic he really likes is the *Pooch Café.* Ranse told me that this particular comic is about a group of dogs that hates cats and whose main objective is to catapult them all into the sun. At the time, we had two cats, so I began reading it, but quickly lost interest.

I know Ranse looks at and likes to read all of the comics. I think a lot of men enjoy reading them and maybe even a select few like *Mary Worth,* but I wonder if they also like women's magazines. Once I began receiving *The Christian Working Woman* in the mail. I hadn't ordered it. When I inquired about it, my husband said, "Oh, I got that off the Internet."

"Why?"

"I like the articles."

"And why is *my* name on the magazine?"

"I couldn't put my name on it."

Now, my man is not effeminate. He's a strapping six-foot-three and weighs around 210, some of which he's usually trying to lose. His hair is almost white now that he's 80; he wears a mustache and goatee, but does have a feminine side. He's sensitive, cares about people, likes to cook and grocery shop, and can also repair anything, so he's an all-around-type guy.

So, getting back to the subject. Where I once ignored the comics, I'm back reading them again; and I guess it's good for a married couple to discuss something light like that while lounging in bed enjoying their morning coffee, rather than talking about the more serious world events in the newspaper.

# Uninvited Guests

*By Bil Fuhrer*

---

F. Scott Fitzgerald wrote: *The test of first-rate intelligence is the ability to hold two opposing ideas in mind and still retain the ability to function.*

> *Headline:* **700-mile border fence moves closer to completion as US-Mexico border is secured**
> *Headline:* **U.S. Senator Diane Feinstein tours tunnel dug from Tijuana to San Diego**

I don't have time to read beyond the headlines. I have a gopher problem. They're destroying our yard. Last year, I dealt with them by simply ignoring the furry little creatures until they finally left, or so I thought. Apparently they took up residence at the rear of the property and have been frolicking and you know what-ing there ever since. There's probably a herd of the pesky incestuous little miners back there by now. It's impossible to know how many because they stay underground, except when they push little piles of evidence to the surface of our manicured lawn and kill the bushes by gnawing the roots.

We are taught to love all God's creatures. This includes gophers and even the scores of spiders who decorate our patio each morning with shimmering dew covered webs.

"Look at all the spiders out here on the patio. Big ones, too. Can't you get rid of them?" barks my wife.

---

I lower the paper and slide my reading glasses down on my nose. "They are God's creatures, too. We should not disturb them. Besides, they help control the bugs."

"Yeah? Well those gophers have no redeeming virtues. What are you going to do about them? They're digging up the whole yard."

She's right, my wife. I have ignored this problem, pretending it didn't exist, they didn't exist, and now I have come to one of those crossroads in life. I have to decide between staying true to a core belief – respect for all living things – and snuffing out the destructive little bastards because they won't leave on their own. But Fitzgerald's profound insight doesn't help me get rid of the gophers. I want them to just go away, back to the fertile fields from whence they came or perhaps to the neighbor's yard – preferably the one to the east. I can no longer ignore the problem.

A lot of advice is available on what to do about gophers:

Mathew: "Use *Gopher Gone*. One teaspoon in each hole and you'll never see them again."

Mark: "Don't ever use a poison like *Gopher Gone*. The poor little creatures die a slow, painful, horrible death. They often come to the surface and stagger around where you can witness their tragic demise. Instead, set a gopher trap at the entrance to their hole. The trap springs shut on its nose and it suffocates in minutes. Then you pull the trap out with the gopher attached and dump it in the trash. It's more humane."

Luke: "Don't use a nose trap. Use a box trap. Capture them alive then transport the frightened critters to an open field somewhere far away. Don't release them in your neighbor's yard because they'll just come back."

*Headline:* **Volunteers organize along Mexican border in Arizona and California to monitor illegal crossings. They call themselves The Minutemen.**

Sierra is a hunter. She is my daughter Julie's gentle and loving Husky who lives to run free and chase squirrels and rabbits in our local mountains. Once, she even caught a mallard duck in her backyard. Julie suggests Sierra visit us for a day, and assures me this descendant of Jack London's Buck will scare the gophers away forever, guaranteed. Why not?

After the usual excited wagging and rubbing, we lead Sierra to the crime scene where, without hesitation, she is on scent with her nose in a hole and her wagging tail curled over her back.

"See? This is gonna work, Dad. She's a very good hunter. Those gophers will be so frightened they will leave and never return. I'll be back this evening to pick her up."

I walk Julie to her car, then return to the yard to see how the hunt is progressing. Sierra is digging furiously in the middle of the manicured lawn and has already gone down two feet. This Husky hunter has become a K-9 backhoe. Dirt flies furiously from between her hind legs as I approach. She is in Husky heaven and excited to be demonstrating her *Call of the Wild* instincts. I drag my enthusiastic minute-mutt away from her prey, wipe her paws and take her home. She has done more damage to my lawn in two minutes than my gopher family did in two or maybe three generations. This cure is worse than the disease.

*Headline:* **Undocumented immigrant population now exceeds eleven million**.

So here I sit, knowing my problem will not go away without action. I feel compassion for the furry little critters but at the same time I want to wring their disruptive, destructive little necks with my bare hands 'til their eyes bug out and they expire.

As Fitzgerald suggests, I am able to hold these two opposing ideas, empathy and strangulation, simultaneously in my mind. Now what?

# Broken Mirror

*By Lloyd Hill*

for Steve Kowit, anti-war poet


Nineteen fifties  18 and19 year old men join
military reserve units to avoid being drafted at 20

I join Army Reserve in 1956
marry, have two children, buy a house
        1960's  Communist Russia threatens US
Berlin Wall Cuban-Missile Crisis

President Kennedy calls my unit to active duty
I hear this first on the radio at home
     son toddling around living room
baby daughter in arms     wife in kitchen

294th Engineering Corps hazardous-duty unit
   learn to kill people and destroy property
Train with dangerous men and demolition
among the guns   live ammo  tanks   barges
underwater diving  cut air hoses  TNT
mustard gas    I'm learning to die too

Live in barracks   army owns me full time
Government Issue 19 542 68
disposable soldier low wage slave
follow orders or go to brig

no privacy yet lonely
    stressed life in constant peril

On Fort Baker phone she tells me
        there are other men

Finally    Honorable Discharge 1963
        A letter of thanks
from Secretary of the Army Cyrus Vance

Come home to empty house for sale
  Climb out of deep depression
Get sick quit smoking    drinking
Army habit's gone but a divorced vet
owing child support looking
 in a broken mirror

# Night Life

*By Lloyd Hill*

Awake in bed   eyes closed   trying to sleep but kangaroo brain
won't quit   poetry ideas bounce about and daytime events
bound through the outback   that jerk with Harley decals and
handicap plates on his Silverado who blocks the garage while
he motorcycles around town doesn't seem crippled to me   I
guess California gives handicapped to anyone   waning
crescent and Venus bright in evening sky a poem?   beautiful
but overdone   write a piece that defies meaning   most poems
in *The New Yorker* are unintelligible   difficult sells in top
markets   study who and what sells   study poetry?   you
don't study poetry   you read it and enjoy it   or not   then you
read more   let your mind gel and see what comes out   damn
neighbor who smokes in the walkway between our units
smoke pours into my place   thirty stinking butts in outside
ashtray   gross   she's not looking so good these days
maybe she'll get sick and move   good thing my thoughts
don't have to be politically correct   should I move my savings
account from Chase Bank to American Express?   triple the
interest   but American Express has no building   it's in the
cloud   most everything is in the cloud these days   virtual
dollars   bitcoins next?   you think Chase has your money in
their vault?   no, but at least they have a building with tellers
too stressful to fuss with banks for a few hundred dollars over
a few years   getting old   can't take it with me   don't look at
the clock   damn it's only 2am   get up and read poetry for a

while    last time I did that I was up all night    crusty next day
long winter nights    no TV no internet    spartan life so as not
to detract from living    comic books my first artistic love
wanted to be a cartoonist    drew hundreds of stories with
captions    but dad said no future there    now with graphic
novels and movies    who knew?    no future in poetry they say
but who knows    look at Billy Collins    Damocles' Sword    a
symbol of dread    what's those marks above letters that mean
possessive    or missing letters    think man    check *Strunk and
White*    oh yeah    apostrophe    the more I learn the less I know
for sure    I've rehashed these thoughts too many times    an
endless tape loop    counting thoughts    should have been an
accountant    instead    I'm a poet who counts    ha    new
thoughts welcome    old thoughts not    driving fast downhill in
a red '63 Chevy with no brakes    whoa    must have fallen
asleep    but awake again    maybe I'll get up and walk in the
morning dark    look for constellations    maybe get inspired
maybe write a poem    maybe write this poem.

# Alma Street

*By Linda Smith*

O UR summer days on Alma Street were lazy and long. We'd swim at Max Myers playground in the big public pool or splash around in the little wading pool set up on the patio. A sudden shower would find us running barefoot, arms and faces turned towards the sky. Hopscotch, drawn in the middle of the street with yellow chalk was a game played by the girls.

Nights were spent outside eating a pretzel or cherry vanilla water ice from Bob's Water Ice truck. All the kids gathered on someone's landing and steps as the boys scared us with their ghost stories. Then we'd play Twenty Questions before my mom, the Kierney's mom, and one by one, all the moms called us in for bed.

But on one particular day, July 27, 1961, summer meant something else too. Helen and I played in the little pool. She sat in the shallow water, legs stretched in front of her. I watched goose bumps on her arms melt. The hose lay on the cement close enough for us to refill water we splashed onto each other and onto the ground. Bees buzzed around the red and pink rose bushes that bordered the patio. I sniffed in the flowers' sweet smell.

"It's my turn," we heard Jimmy, youngest of the five Kierny kids next door, say. He bounced a ball to one of his older sisters. Their shorthaired, yellow dog Bonnie, barked each time the ball hit the pavement.

"Time to empty the pool and come in for lunch," Mom yelled through the open front room window.

"Ahhh, already?" No answer from Mom, so we pulled the plugs.

Helen stuck her big toe with the chipped pink nail polish onto a hole. "Put your toe on the other one."

"Okay, let's not go in yet." We were eight years old and giggled a lot. Playing with Helen was fun. But once lunch was over, her mother would probably stop by and take her home.

"How come you hardly ever come to my house?"

"Oh, my mom says your brothers are too wild."

*Can't do much about that.* I stared at our feet and watched the water drain.

Without warning, a deafening sound blasted through the air, like ten cars backfiring at the same time. Helen and I froze. Everything stopped. We couldn't hear Bonnie bark, a baby cry or a mom yell at their kid. Looking down I saw the remaining water jiggle and heard the windows above us rattle. Helen and I looked at each other and screamed. Her eyes were wide and her hands covered her mouth.

My two older brothers flew out of the house. They took the first five steps to the landing in one jump. My jaw dropped as I watched them run down our neighbor's lawn and disappear. Half a dozen kids passed our house as they ran towards that sound.

"What was that?" I yelled as they whizzed by.

Mom shouted, "Get inside the house, now!"

Helen and I exchanged glances, her eyebrows raised. As if reading her mind, I silently agreed that sitting down to a bowl of tomato soup at that moment was out of the question. The only thing I wanted to do was run down the street too.

We took off with wet hair and bare feet. I looked for my brothers. Kids and adults were running from all directions.

A crowd had gathered in the middle of the next block of Alma Street. Nobody said anything for a while. The faces I saw looked as surprised and dazed as I felt. We passed three teens who stood on the hood of a car. "Yeah, he's gotta be connected to the Mafia," one of them said.

Helen squeezed my hand and pointed to shattered glass that littered the street. I kept my eyes on the black tar after that, careful not to step on any glass. We'd been so caught up in the excitement, we forgot to put on flip-flops or grab towels. Water from the bottom of my soaked black and white bathing suit dripped down my legs.

Looking up I saw living room windows shattered on several houses on one side of the street. It was my side of the street only a block away. Even though I felt nervous, confused and scared, there was no place else I wanted to be.

"Holy crap! The hood of his car flew halfway down the street and is up here on the roof," a teenage boy yelled.

Standing on the outside of the crowd on tiptoes, I peeked through spaces between the heads of people bunched close together. Through the smoke that hung in the air, I tried to see something, anything. There was a terrible odor, like hardboiled eggs on a hot summer day that had been in a picnic basket for too long.

All I saw were the backs of boys' necks and heads, their hair greased down and cut short, jutting out of plaid or checkered shirts. I hopped from one foot to the other because the hot tar burned my feet. A couple of people coughed and my eyes stung.

Someone who stood closer to the scene said, "The guy's name was Richie Blaney. He was turning over the ignition in his car and it exploded. He exploded."

Two older boys rode past us and screeched to a halt. One of them said, "Man, we just got back from swimming at Maxie's. Look at this."

The other answered, "I know. That's Mr. Blaney's car. He always parked it right between second and third base."

"We woulda been playing stick ball right here if it hadn't been so hot."

"Yeah and he probably would have moved his car so we could set up bases; he was nice like that."

"Jeez, we could of got blown up too."

Another kid shouted from a rooftop, "I found one of his fingers."

Someone else yelled, "His Timex watch is still ticking!"

The eldest Kierny kid, Brandan, came over to where we were standing. He had a goofy cockeyed smile on his pimply face. He looked directly at Helen and me. "I got to look right into the back seat of the car. I saw his head with strands of hair drenched in blood. They looked just like spaghetti!"

That made me feel sick. Brandan looked at me, his blue eyes dancing and yellow teeth showing. He laughed his older, mean-boy laugh.

Helen's mother found us. "Come on, it's time to go home now." She pulled Helen's hand out of mine.

Helen looked back at me as she was being dragged off. "Come over later, okay?"

"Okay, see ya later."

I looked around one more time. Boys were pushing each other, people were laughing, talking about how crazy it all was. But we weren't at a block party or a picnic. Feeling a little dizzy, I stood silent.

It was time for me to leave, too. Walking home alone, I tried to understand why someone would be blown up. I wondered if Mr. Blaney had been dressed in a white shirt and nice slacks. Maybe he even wore a tie, like on the commercials for Timex watches. I thought they were expensive. It was something my dad didn't have.

Did he just walk out of his house in the middle of this hot day, get into his car, turn over the ignition and…just like that, his life was over? Wow. And now his kids would never see him again, and neighborhood kids he probably didn't even know were finding his body parts.

At home I went upstairs to lie down. Picking up my stuffed bunny rabbit and bear, I hugged them close, shut my eyes and tried to forget what I just saw.

# A Day On The Beach

*By Rebecca Johnson*

WALKING on the beach I spot a handsome man sitting on the sand with expensive looking shoes next to him. I sit nearby; *he might be someone with money I could marry.*

"What's your name? Do you come to this beach often?" I ask. *What a lame thing to say.*

"Maurice. Not too often, are you here a lot?"

"Not a lot but it is pleasant here. Would you like to dance with me?"

"I don't usually think of dancing on the beach, but I'm willing to try it. What's your name?"

"Laura."

Maurice stands up and we dance near the water's edge. The tide's coming in pretty fast. We start getting swept along in the rising water against our will, and it's now harder to stay on our feet, so we soon retreat to our beach towels on the sand.

I say, "Would you like to go to the bar on the boardwalk for some wine?"

"I don't have time now I'm meeting my wife for lunch soon," Maurice says.

My heart sank. "Oh you're married."

"I am married, but I could be open to having a girlfriend," he offers.

"That sounds a bit too crowded for me. I think I'll pass on that," I reply sounding disappointed.

"Well, if you're sure you feel that way, I have to be going. I enjoyed dancing with you."

With that, Maurice turns and walks away.

I start scanning the beach and spot a handsome lifeguard approaching. I dash into the water and swim farther out, over my head in the hope that this lifeguard will swim after me, sweep me up in his arms and take me home.

Except I haven't noticed how strong the current is. I start drifting, only to bump into a teenager floating on a rubber raft. He sees me struggling and tells me he will tow me along if I hold on to the side.

*Where are we going now? I'm getting even farther away from my dreamboat lifeguard.*

"Hey, kid," I say, "could you just help me back toward shore where I can stand in the water?"

"OK, I can do that," says the kid.

Back on shore, I scan the beach for my lifeguard, but only spot another lifeguard. *Maybe he'll be just as dreamy.*

I head out into the water again, swimming furiously to get out over my head. When I'm out far enough, I start waving and wailing. I see the lifeguard throw himself in the water.

*Oh, I'm going to be saved by a dreamboat, and we'll go off together into the future.*

*Oh no, it's not my handsome lifeguard, it's a big strapping girl.*

*There's got to be an easier way to find my dreamboat husband. I'm heading to the bar on the boardwalk. Maybe I'll have better luck there.*

# Senses

*By Tim Calaway*

Forgotten now

a first love

of many years ago

 heightened my senses

to hear hummingbird whispers,

to see dandelion smiles.

Age has left my senses colder

as it has made me older

not without hope

an ember still glows

And once more

I'll listen for

The whispers of hummingbirds.

# Recipe

*By Linda Smith*

Nobody made blintzes like you did,
nobody could.

I wouldn't eat a blintz
for years after you passed.
not until Aunt Mildred shared your recipe.

She, following you about the kitchen,
observing your every move,
translating words spoken in Yiddish,
approximating, into measurements,
a bissel of this and a bissel of that.

Attempting to capture on paper,
your great confidence and style.

If we could bottle that, she said,
we'd all be rich today.

I wish my friends could have
seen you in the kitchen.
carrying worn cotton table cloths,
huge sacks of flour,
a heavy Bauer bowl.

Fire burning beneath
three cast iron skillets,
you maneuvered between them
all at once.

Flipping paper-thin crepes
with bare fingers,
you never got burned, or tore one.

Turning our humble row-house kitchen
into a place that produced, mouth watering,
food for a hundred, all day long.

Rarely would you sit down, and I never saw you
tire, forget what you were doing,
or miss a beat.

I miss you Grandmom.

And much as my friends like
the blintzes I make,
I only hope they do you
justice.

# Freedom from FEAR

*By Dave Schmidt*

From distant past to present time
*Fear* has stalked and haunted Mankind
With degrees of control and suffering realized
*Freedom* and happiness are victimized
Concern, panic, dread, anxiety and worries
Fear wears many disguises

From immediate causes unknown
*Fear* continues to work its will
Attachment and uncertainty together, evil duo
With *Freedom* sacrificed, spells trouble
If fear of flying, learn about safety – uncertainty to counter
If fear of loss, let go – attachment to counter

From pain realized, apply more steps
*Fear* as intruder into our life not denied
Courage to face fear, do what is necessary
Then *Freedom* from its grip, not far away
If fear in battle, just push forward
If fear intense, massage the heart as a sore shoulder

From not understanding this dis-ease
*Fear* cleverly engages in mind control
Paralysis of analysis or negative thoughts, breeds fear
*Freedom* achieved by correcting the mental process

If afraid of past or future, thinking won't change
If obsessed with courses of action, make decision, not to change

Now with fear well managed, not ready to end its reign
Still a role to play in an unenlightened society.

# The Circle of Life

*By Mary Carnes*

SUSAN finished drying her hands on the hand towel, and when she turned, spotted the small worm-like creature about one and a half inches long on the floor by the shower. It crawled ever so slowly. Her first impulse was to step on it but she became fascinated by its movement. Grabbing a magnifying glass from the computer room, she got down on her knees, bent over, and put the glass down next to the crawling thing to get a closer look. It had tiny legs coming from its blackish/brown body. For about a minute, she sat on the floor and watched it creep along.

Then, deciding not to waste any more time, Susan stood back up. That's when she spotted the spider.

The eight-legged spider was small and black, not the daddy long-legs type she usually saw in the bathroom. As it spun toward the worm with legs, it came down the shower's glass door moving toward its prey at a fast pace. Susan did not see the web at first, as it was practically invisible, until the worm jerked backward and was lifted into the air. The tiny plant-eating scavenger curled up, struggled, and got loose from the mesh structure. It escaped only to be caught again and again by the spinning web. The worm was in a fight for its life and the spider was just as determined to get its meal.

With pieces of the delicate thread hanging from its body, the worm continually escaped. Finally, the spider lost interest in the fight and retreated back up its web. Bravo, Susan thought, as the jointed invertebrate inched away.

She didn't have the heart to kill it after seeing it so valiantly defend its life, but Susan didn't want it in the bathroom either. She grabbed a piece of toilet paper, gently scooped up the tiny creature, opened the front door and tossed it into the bush bearing red flowers, hoping it would live a bit longer on the outside.

The next morning, her husband, Tommy, informed her that last night he had spotted a Daddy Long-legs in the sink of the same bathroom.

"Well, what did you do with it?" Susan asked.

"You know how I hate to kill spiders," Tommy said. "I picked it up and tossed it into the bush outside the front door." Susan then told him what had taken place in the bathroom and exclaimed, "That's where I tossed the centipede!"

Tommy looked at her and wryly commented. "I guess the circle of life continues."

\* \* \*

Later, when Susan looked it up on the Internet, she read that what she saw was a many-legged arthropod called the millipede. Susan first thought it was its cousin, the centipede. Both it and its cousin are related to shrimp, crawfish and lobster. The name "millipede" is a compound word formed from the Latin roots *milli* ("thousand") and *ped* ("foot"). Despite their name, millipedes do not have 1,000 legs, although a rare species has up to 750. Common species have between 36 and 400 legs. They come in different sizes and colors and their bodies are made up of segments, most of which have two pair of legs. There are 10,000 species and the average lifespan is 7 years.

As a defense mechanism, it curls up in a tight ball to protect its legs. Many species emit poisonous liquid secretions, usually harmless to humans but can cause pain and itching. Some places in Asia do eat centipedes. For instance, in Beijing, China's Donghuamen Night Market, one can find bugs, insects, spiders, centipedes and many other species eaten for protein and street food.

# Post Manumission

*By Joe Torricelli* _____

With the Thirteenth Amendment

Ole 'Massa' lost his slaves.

With tobacco he got them back.

Smoke addicts they returned

brown, lily white, n' black

# Another Sunset

*By Paul Ford*

---

A N attractive elderly lady had herself wheeled out onto the rear lanai of a white colonial convalescent home. Malia, a pretty young nurse's aide, positioned the chair so that Elizabeth could see beyond the palm trees to the sky over the yacht club.

"The bay is calm this evening. Enjoy the sunset, but don't get chilled, okay?"

The lady smiled and patted Malia's hand. She began humming a song. Lost in her thoughts, she was unaware an elderly man had wheeled himself up about two feet away from her.

Without preamble he asked, "What's that song you're humming?"

Elizabeth slowly turned her head. He was as old as she, but maybe healthier, judging by the color in his cheeks and his ramrod posture. She felt he was being rude and decided to be brief.

"It's a simple melody."

"That's the title?"

"Sir, I believe it's properly called 'Play a Simple Melody.'"

"I'm sorry if I'm bothering you." He turned his chair as if ready to leave.

"No, no. I'm sorry if I was being abrupt. People mistakenly mislabel the song. I feel strongly about it. My father used to sing it to me and my brother when we were

---

young. He was a Marine." She paused. "He died on Guadalcanal."

"I was a Marine. My name is Robert."

The lady smiled. "Not Bob or Bobby or Rob?" she teased. "That's very formal, Robert."

"So, I've been told. Once, long ago, I knew a girl who said that very same thing. Then it bothered me. When you said it, I wasn't bothered. I wondered why."

"I guess at our age, some things cease to bother us, don't you think?" She gazed across the short span separating them. "My name is Elizabeth."

"Not Betty, Bette, Liz, or Eliza?"

"Touché. Tell me, do you have a story to go along with this girl you mentioned? What was her name?"

"There is a story. Strangely, I don't remember her name. We met at the Marine base across the bay. Her brother asked me to spend a day with her. He had some squadron flying to attend to. I guess he trusted me."

"Was he right about trusting you, Robert?"

"Sure, I was a shy young Marine." He thought for a moment. "I called her brother 'Shute.' "

"Was he a good shooter?"

"That's not the reason. His name was Shuttenburg. He was my roommate."

"And you remember that and not the girl's name?" Elizabeth looked at Robert with increasing interest.

"Maybe it will come to me. Anyway, she arrived and Shute brought her to the Bachelor Officers Quarters and introduced us. My first impression of her was that she was preoccupied about something, pensive, maybe, or sad."

"Was she pretty?"

"She was cute. Dark hair cut in a page boy style and bright blue eyes, but as I said, something was bothering her. I felt awkward. She wanted to do some snorkeling, so I grabbed some gear and I drove us over to Hanauma Bay."

"Yes, I know the place, idyllic and romantic."

"Yes, a long walk down from the parking lot, but definitely worth the trip. We were the only people there."

"Now the parking lot is full from dawn to dusk," Elizabeth said.

"Yes, so I'm told. Anyway, we snorkeled and watched colorful fish in the coral reef. She wanted to check out all the reef areas."

"So, she was a true aficionado."

"Yes. Interestingly, as we snorkeled, her sadness dissipated. Often, she pointed out particularly colorful fish to me. Then later we frolicked and swam until we could hardly move. As we lay in the sand afterwards, she kissed me on the cheek."

"And, of course, being a man, you wanted more."

"I believe I was content with the kiss on the cheek. Even though she seemed to rid herself of the earlier sadness, I still felt that she was vulnerable."

"You could have put your arm around her. Maybe she needed comforting."

Robert nodded. "You seem to have an inordinate interest, Elizabeth."

"I was a young girl once. Sometimes young girls need comforting. Does the story end there?"

"Yes. I took her back to the base. Shute had finished flying and was going to take her to dinner that evening."

The horizon reddened as the daylight receded. Flat sparse clouds slowly moved over the bay and the ocean beyond.

Elizabeth remarked, "My favorite time of day."

"I prefer sunrises," Robert countered. "If I'm awake, I can quietly greet the sun and celebrate another day."

Elizabeth grimaced as if experiencing a pang of pain. Robert noticed, but didn't speak. He looked away allowing her the dignity of dealing with whatever discomfort she might be experiencing.

The moments passed. A plantation fan whirred overhead.

Elizabeth asked, "Did you try to contact this girl? Maybe ask her brother for an address so you could write to her?"

"I did. He told me that she was having boyfriend trouble, which further confirmed my thoughts that she was vulnerable."

Malia returned and stood behind Elizabeth, ready to wheel her back inside.

"Will you be out here tomorrow evening, Robert?" Elizabeth asked.

"Yes, same time, same place. Good night, Elizabeth."

Robert sat awhile longer. Hearing a jet passing over, he imagined a well executed, but abrupt landing on the short runway at the Marine air station. Saddened, he rotated his wheel chair and headed indoors.

The next evening, Elizabeth was wheeled out on the lanai in time for another sunset. Robert wasn't there. But then, a short time later, he appeared, wheeling up close to her.

"I was afraid you wouldn't show up, Robert."

"I was on my way, but was informed by a nurse that I hadn't taken my evening medication."

"Yes, we must take our medication, mustn't we?"

Clouds obscured the evening sky. A storm was approaching the bay.

"Did you ever wonder what happened to this mysterious girl?"

Robert's face clouded. "I saw her again a year later at Shute's memorial at the base's chapel."

Elizabeth turned her wheel chair slightly away from Robert.

He noticed, but continued: "Shute had flown in too fast and overshot the runway. He died on impact."

Elizabeth sucked in a deep breath.

"I saw his sister and, I assume, her mother at the funeral service. There was a crowd of his friends lined up to offer condolences. When I came to Shute's sister, I touched her hand. She just nodded, but didn't look up, so I just moved on."

"A shame you didn't hold her hand and say her name."

With the clouds gathering, the air became damp and cool. Malia came out and hurriedly wheeled Elizabeth inside before she and Robert had a chance to say good-by.

Later, an orderly helped Robert into bed. His thoughts went back to that magical day at Hanauma Bay with Shute's sister. Suddenly, he remembered her name and thought how extraordinary life could be. Then his thoughts turned to his everlasting friendship with Shute and the experiences they had shared on Oahu.

That night, Elizabeth experienced increasing pain in her abdominal area. Unable to sleep, she thought about that day with a shy marine all those years ago. She had ached for him to hold her tight, but it wasn't to be.

The next morning, while Robert was enjoying the sunrise, Elizabeth was taken to a nearby hospital. After an examination, her physician said she had a growth in her uterus.

"The surgeon will determine if it is malignant or benign," Dr. Samuelson said.

When Elizabeth awoke, her doctor told her the operation was successful and the growth was benign.

She slept on and off during bouts of pain and strange dreams. Awakening in the early evening, a nurse told her she had a visitor.

Not knowing what to expect, Robert smiled tentatively. When he saw Elizabeth's smile, he knew she was recuperating nicely. Malia wheeled his chair up to her bed.

"Hi, Beth."

Her smile broadened. "Hello, Robert. At one point in my life, just as you had suggested to me all those years ago, I decided to use the name my parents gave me."

"My close friends call me Bob." He reached over and held her hand while the sun set.

# Before I Sleep

*By Wallace Watson*

Next to you my
Body can not tell
Where you begin or
Where I end

We are
One
Our bodies and souls
Slip into each other

And rest in another
Dimension
One lightning bolt electrifying
The cosmos

# Changeling

*By Harry Field*

With tangled locks, wind-lifted, copper red against the hot
  blue August haze,
She seemed a wild thing, standing knee deep in purple
  heather.
Her gold flecked, rain-grey eyes conjured a vague unease,
For she soon must learn to wear a proper snood,
To sew, to sing, dance, and play the lute.

They sat her on a green silk chair and brushed her curls to
  splendor,
Taught her shallow arts then left her toying with a tapestry.
In the golden cast of noon she nodded o'er the sun-dial,
Drowsily wondering why yellow roses surpassed the creamy
  ones,
And if her faery prince would ever come.

Secure, she slumbered, artless and pale, a marble nymph
  among cypress,
And in her dream trooped airy, elfin things.
Whose clamoring voices woke echoes in her heart of a magic
  land,

Familiar, like wraiths, haunting still,

From a childhood long forgotten.


She started, waked by pixie songs, but knew no fright,

As nearby beckoned a tall, black-armored Prince,

Astride a fire-breathed, green and silver dragon.

They bore her swift away beyond a sun-specked sea,

To dwell in Faeryland 'til Time is o'er.

A changeling child reclaimed by Faery folk.

# Summer Camp 1974

*By Linda Smith*

"WHY don't you apply for a camp counselor job at the Y?" Jill asked, looking at me through square-shaped glasses, her green eyes intense. "That's where I'm working this summer. Hey, you can use me as a reference."

I sat cross-legged on her bed, my back against the concrete wall. Jill and Tina, friends from Unitarian Church in Detroit, shared the dorm room we were crammed into. "Well, yeah, of course they hired you. You can do every craft known to mankind and play several instruments. Not to mention dance and choreography. What have I got to offer?"

"Oh, come on, you can teach cooking, drama, and I'll pair up with you to teach macramé together. Or, I'll teach you macramé and just pass it on." She looked at me with those wise green eyes again. "You only need to be one step ahead of the kids."

"Hmmm, I do need a summer job. And it would be fun to work together. Let me think about it."

"Okay, but don't think for too long. Everybody's applying for work-study jobs now."

"How about you, Tina?" I asked. "Are you looking for a job?"

"Didn't I tell you? I'm moving to New York. To paint."

"You guys are so talented." *How'd I wind up with such creative friends?*

The first few days of inner-city youth camp at Grand Rapid's YWCA came and went. The most remarkable thing about them for me was all the energy it took to keep my insecurities at bay.

Each class had no more than ten girls, between the ages of seven and twelve. A few of the girls looked either older or younger, but no one said anything. The teachers, along with the administrators, knew it was a safe place to send young girls each day. There was food, a bus-trip outing once a week, and supervision. If a parent had lied about the age of their kid, we'd been told by the Director to overlook it. *No problem.*

On the first Thursday of the summer program, we went to Duck Lake State Park. I was as excited as the kids, because I'd never been there. Leaving the city behind to visit a beach was fine with me.

We boarded and I sat in an aisle seat right about in the middle of the bus. The window seat next to me was available. A little girl I hadn't met before climbed onto my lap.

"Well, hello." I tried to hide my surprise and looked at her. "Do you want to sit on the seat next to the window?"

"No." She looked at me. "I'm too short. I won't be able to see anything."

"Oh, okay. So, you're gonna sit here, on my lap?" I wasn't prepared for this.

"Yep." She made herself comfortable and then stared straight ahead.

"Huh, alright, well, I'm Linda."

"Hi." Turning her face towards me again she said, "Everyone calls me Piglet."

I giggled. "Nice to meet you Piglet." Smiling, I took in her ebony colored skin and almond-shaped brown eyes. I couldn't tell how old this tiny girl was; she was very thin and small.

We rode along for a while. The two of us sat in silence. I wondered if this was odd, or if I should encourage her more to sit on a seat, or what. Some of the older girls told stories in quiet voices, and the yellow Bluebird bus hummed its way along. *This might be a good time to catch a nap.*

After a few moments of dozing, I felt Piglet's small hands on my cheeks. She'd turned around and when I opened my eyes, she was staring straight at me.

"Is you mulatto?"

Taken a bit off guard, I remembered the first time I'd heard that word. I was about nine and we were down the shore for summer vacation in Atlantic City. Two teenage girls were in the ocean near me. They'd been whispering to each other and looking in my direction. I was hoping they would come talk to me because I was bored and lonely. Then one of them did.

"Hi, I'm Gina and that's my friend Trish." Trish waved. "We were just wondering something…"

*Wondering about me?*

"Um, well, we wanted to ask you, um, are you mulatto?"

"What? I don't know what that is."

"Oh, never mind," she'd said and started to swim away.

"Hey, wait, just tell me what that word means."

"Okay," she moved through the water closer to me again. "So, we were just wondering if your Daddy was like darker than your Mommy is…"

I stared at her and thought for a moment. "Oh, cause I'm so brown." Looking at her, I rubbed my arm. "No, I'm not … that. My mom says I just tan well in the summer."

"Okay, thanks." Gina and Trish both swam away.

Although maybe I shouldn't have been, I was surprised when Piglet asked me that same question, ten years later. "No, no I'm not," I said shaking my head. "My grandparents were all from Eastern Europe; Poland, Romania, Russia. Do you know where Europe is?"

"Hmmph," Piglet said as she pushed herself off my lap and onto the seat by the window.

"Piglet, why don't you leave that lady alone?" one of the older girls said.

"Hmmph," Piglet crossed her thin arms against her chest.

I wasn't sure what to say next and decided that taking a nap was still a good idea.

Before long, I felt someone, Piglet, climb onto my lap again. I opened my eyes. She'd placed her hands firmly on my cheeks and put her forehead up against mine.

"You is mulatto. You just doesn't want to say." There was a note of anger in her voice. Maybe hurt too, and disappointment.

"No." I shook my head. "I'm not. But if I were, I would say." I looked at her for a moment, felt her measuring my words. "And you know what Piglet?" I paused and felt my heart race. "I would be proud to say." And here, I tried not to let my voice crack. My throat hurt because I was forcing myself not to cry. "I would be very proud to say."

We sat like that for a bit longer, just looking into each other's eyes. I noticed now that the only sound was the dull roar of the bus.

Finally, Piglet released me and rested her head and face on my chest. Still trying not to cry, I swallowed and kissed the top of her head. I looked around and saw the Director/bus driver's eyes and face in the rear view mirror. It looked like she had been quietly crying – her cheeks were flushed, her eyes looked watery.

Needing that nap now more than ever, I closed my eyes once more and let the drone of the bus take me away.

# Enchantress

*By Tim Calaway*

Looking at your picture

Wishing I'd known you then

At a different point in time

Not this crossroads of separated years.

Crooked smile shyly hinting

Of the person you would be.

Glistening dark eyes drawing me in,

But not far enough, not now.

Too late to have that chance.

Homecoming Queen of 1946,

Wrapped around a candlestick

Stored for decades in grandpa's attic

Waiting to be freed

To enchant once more.

# Maggie

*By Erika Toraya*                                    December 3, 2013

ER heart has an abnormal beat. She has excessive gas in her stomach. Her body scabs reveal an over-reaction to flea bites, which may mean her immune system is not functioning well. And, it could be cancer.

These words reach my ears in slow motion and trickle down to my heart, filling it with sadness. Maggie is my precious, petite, fluffy-haired, princess. Nestled in her carrier box, she stares up at me with her beautiful green eyes, set against her white whiskered nose and tiger-striped coat. We share a look of recognition from our special bond of 16 years together. As I cry on the ride back home, she begins to sadly answer back in long, sweet "meow's."

She may recover just fine after her medication is complete, and hopefully the results from the test are negative of any death-causing problems. Then, there will be no more expensive tests and she will live many more years. I know some indoor cats live well into their 20's and Maggie needs to be one of them.

I love how Maggie curls herself into the hollow of my body when we nap on the couch. Her motor-boat purr clearly expresses love and comfort. I reminisce over the couple of times she returned home spider-webbed and panicked after escaping out of the house for an adventure. She knew where her refuge was, and I was glad I didn't lose her.

When I first brought her home as a seven-week old kitten, I didn't have a name picked out. My roommate brilliantly offered in her New Zealand accent, "Why don't you nime ur after your mum?" The year prior, I had lost the original Maggy. Mom had died and my world turned upside down. I could at least have a little reminder of her in my new kitten. It would be very ironic to name her after my mom who had always hated cats. The thought made me smile. This can be our little inside joke. Would that piss her off or make her smile? Ah well, Maggie it is! A little different spelling to give each her identity, of course.

Strange how this feline has a familiarity about her. Her personality is similar to my mom's in several ways. They are both great at nurturing and cuddling, but only when in the mood. Rulers of the house. Beautiful and spunky. Small but mighty. Like when Maggie's seven-pound frame hisses, "You stupid dog! Who brought you into my house? Haven't you been informed? I rule around here!" Vocal and finicky.

In two days, it will be December 5th, the anniversary of my mom's death. The reminder of my loss approaches me each year like a freight train eager to reach its station. Now, hearing the news of Maggie the same week is too close a connection. I am overcome with a desperate un-acceptance at the possibility of losing Maggie and that little piece of my mom that I have in her.

Having lost motivation to write for more than two months, my grief pierces me with a desire to write. The words relate reasons, tell tales, and enable emotions. The journey of writing brings me understanding and comfort. Empowerment and healing. Freedom and determination. I know I can be joyful in the spirit of my mom for the 5th of December and gratefully, it does turn out to be a blessed day. Perfect timing even delivers a message from the vet: the test results came back fine.

Having healed from the fleas, things seem much better and she's back to her normal behaviors. She may still have an off-beat heart and over-stimulated digestive system, but hey, at 16 years old, she seems to be doing fine and why try to change things with medications when it seems to be working for her. So we keep truckin'. I'm happy to have her a bit longer. When the time does come, I know that both Maggie and Mama Maggy will always be with me. But, here's lookin' to another eight or nine years, right?

# Nothing for It

*By Avery Kerr*

RUTHIE and I may not have been madly in love to begin with, but we made a solid couple. Honest with one another, we didn't fight much. Squabbles over chores and schedules, but no long-term resentments or explosions. Educated and ambitious, we met through work. Simon and Schuster sent her to my firm for money. When I secured a loan that allowed their large publishing house to buy a small, independent press, Ruth liked the way I handled the matter.

"Al's a real pro," she would say, when she told our story. "Plus, he made sure people didn't lose jobs."

We'd been married for about three years, when she came home in tears after a routine checkup. "The doctor suggests we see a specialist."

"What for?"

"Babies." Ruth dabbed her eyes with a tissue.

During the long interview at the fertility clinic, Ruth surprised me. She'd been keeping track all along, planning our couplings to coincide with fertile days in her cycle.

"She never said that children were so important," I told the doctor.

A few months later Ruth seemed resigned. "My eggs aren't making it far enough to meet up with your wiggly little guys." Even though she insisted the fault was hers, I suspected my wiggly little guys weren't swimming fast enough.

For a short while, we considered adoption, but the lengthy process required time away from our precious careers.

With stressful jobs in the city, both of us suffered long hours, tight deadlines, demanding bosses. Along with other young professionals, we developed a competitive social life that matched our growing salaries. In time, we accepted childlessness as if we had chosen it.

Year after year we succeeded at work, enjoying promotions and reaping big bonuses. Weekends meant reading *The Times* cover to cover and meeting other couples for Sunday brunch. Conversations followed the news; we talked politics and sports, theater and music. Ruthie had a fascination with off-Broadway plays. I developed an interest in jazz. Not quite a power couple, but close.

Ruth started collecting small eighteenth century European oils that cost several thousand dollars each. She displayed several, with gallery lighting, on the living room wall of our Upper East Side apartment. I joined The Brook, a private gentleman's club. Fred Astaire had been a member, so had John F. Kennedy.

At fifty, we considered retirement, but we had no idea how to be anything other than busy New Yorkers. Looking back, we seem selfish, and indulgent. It's hard to pinpoint what changed. Little things at first: opening the refrigerator to find only styrofoam containers of leftovers, tossing wine bottles with fancy labels into the recycling bin, missing family birthday celebrations because of our jobs. The emptiness peeked out, winking, one eye at a time.

"It's always been like this," Ruth said, when I mentioned my discomfort. "But you've just noticed."

One spring Sunday, after eggs and champagne at Beaumarchais, Ruth suggested a stroll. As we wandered through the East Village, she told me about Maggie. "She's a darling, Al." Ruth took my hand. "New to publishing.

Youthful and dewy-eyed, like I used to be." She grabbed my hand a bit harder. "Are you listening?"

"Yes," I said, even though I hadn't been.

"Something special about her. Can we have them over for dinner?"

Now she had my attention. During the course of our nearly twenty year marriage, we'd had dinner guests only twice: my parents, and her brother and his wife. "Okay." I nodded.

"You'll like her husband, too."

"What's he do?"

"Construction."

My eyebrows raised, and my mouth formed a doubtful smirk.

Ruth laughed. "Geez, you're such a snob." She punched my arm lightly. "God forbid we'd have a dinner guest who got his hands dirty with manual labor."

Even though I knew she was kidding, her comment bugged me. Because she was right. I was a snob. About food and wine. People, too. Before I could defend myself, she went on: "Don't worry, sweetie. He's a foreman."

"Oh, good," I said. "Sure, ask them."

Ruth stopped to peer into a window of a children's boutique. "They have a little girl, Tessa."

My wife was staring at a stuffed panda.

"Will she come along?" I asked, even though I knew the answer.

Ruth was right. I did like Jim Donnelly. Maggie, too. And Tess, their four year old, most of all. As soon as the family arrived, we realized that protecting our precious *objets d'art* from the exploring hands of a curious child would be impossible.

"I'm so sorry," Maggie said, when Tess opened our front door so hard that a glass vase toppled from a low shelf.

"We should have called a sitter." Jim caught the vase and handed it to me.

"Nonsense," Ruth said. "Take their coats, Al. And fix drinks. Tessa..." Ruth took her hand. "...come with me." They went into the kitchen. A few minutes later Tess came out wearing a tiny apron. Taking slow steps, she carried a plate and set it down on the coffee table. I stifled a laugh. In all our years together, we'd never eaten anything that resembled these hors d'ouvres.

"What's this?" I asked, and pointed to a Saltine covered with a tangle of orange squiggles.

"An octopus!" Tess clapped her hands. "I made it." When I pretended to be frightened, she giggled. "It's cheese."

Ruth came through the door with another tray that bore stuffed olives, Marcona almonds, and goat brie. "Here we are."

I reached for one of Tessa's decorated crackers. "No thank you, I'm having octopus." My jaw opened wide, and I made a big deal about taking a bite. Pieces of cracker went flying onto the Persian rug. Sticky, salty fake cheddar smeared across my chin.

That night I fell in love twice. Tessa taught me to play. She called me "Pal", and the nickname stuck. And Ruth, my wife, had bought the crackers, spray-can cheese, the child-size apron, and a lovely doll that Tess pretended to feed while the adults conversed. How good we would have been with children.

Over the next two years, the friendship grew. Ruth mentored Maggie at work, showing her how to woo best-selling authors away from other publishing houses. A tricky business that involved contract lawyers and a bit of travel. We spent many weekends at the Donnelly home in Connecticut, learning how to relax. One afternoon Jim showed me his job site, a hotel remodel in Brooklyn. I traded my Italian loafers for work boots.

When Maggie got pregnant, Ruth insisted we retire. "We need to help out, Al. Her folks live clear across the country; his are in Ireland."

I didn't resist. Our lovely apartment seemed sterile compared to the three bedroom house we bought in Newton. Ruth auctioned the paintings; I handed out bottles from my wine collections as farewell gifts. We didn't look back.

Baby Sam arrived, and Maggie took maternity leave. Ruth planted flowers, something she'd always wanted to do. When Tess turned five, the party was at our house. Ruth helped Tess decorate homemade cupcakes with green and pink icing. The following summer Ruth tried a vegetable garden. At harvest time she and Tess practiced cooking. My preference for food prepared in upscale restaurants shifted to curiosity; the journey from connoisseur to guinea pig included eating all their experiments.

When Maggie went back to commuting, the baby spent days in child care. When Jim needed to be out-of-town on business, Tess began to spend several nights a week at our house. It was easier on Maggie. We gave our little princess full reign, including a room of her own. She chose bright pink for the walls; she asked for a canopy bed, and a window seat with purple cushions. I learned about priming and sandpaper; Ruth took up sewing. When Tess started first grade, I drove her to Hawley Elementary. Time should have stopped then.

It's been a year.

"You're lucky," people say when they hear Tess didn't attend Sandy Hook.

But we don't feel lucky. Memorial parks with angel statues and scholarship funds do nothing to lessen our despair. Everything reminds us that we live with the possibility of loss. Like the school building, we are demolished.

Ruth, all knobby knees and elbows, curls into my chest. Small to begin with, she's smaller now. "I weigh the same," she explains. "The spirit shrivels."

Animals in a den, we seek creature comfort. The horrors of each day wait, fangs bared, and we are the prey of our own imaginations. Holding her, I imagine pieces broken from a larger continent, eons ago, straining to reconstruct a map that makes sense.

# My World from A to Z

*By Marion Kahn*

Always attracted to foreign lands where
Beauty and strangers call to me
Charming tour guides and occasional pompous ones
Describe their homelands proudly
Exotic food, bewildering languages
Finnish and Polish challenge the ear
Guatemalan weavers wear back-strap looms
Hungarians, proud of their powerful paprika
Iguassu Falls gush over Brazil and Paraguay
Jewel-like mosaics delight in Bologna
Krakow and Prague, two enchanting cities
Le Lavandou, Bastille Day fireworks
Madrid, bar hopping with a matador
Norway's fishing villages and fjords
Ouzo and ancient Muses cast a spell in Greece
Pyramids and camels when Egypt was peaceful
Queen's English, proper and almost understandable
Romania where my grandparents were born
Snake charmers, belly dancers and Marrakesh mosques
Tapestries and Turkish carpets begging to be bought
Ukrainians, so proud not to be Russian
Villagers welcome us in happy Bhutan
Warm, wistful memories of reunions with friends abroad
Xenophobia was never my problem
Youth, though, has passed me by, and here at home I settle for
Zesty foreign food, foreign visitors, zebras in the local zoo,
        memories.

# Restless Woman

*By Jean E. Taddonio* ———————————

Each time she seeks a change

an aching to be free

she pretends herself a river

raging for the sea


And when she widens into stillness

and the restlessness subsides

she smiles at her impatience

no longer needing her disguise

# On This Day

*By Nancy Foley*

On this day I stand in silence

surrounded by old growth redwoods

some eighteen hundred years old.

Through shafts of muted light

my eyes search for royal crowns

close to three hundred feet above.

I shiver in cold air that

creates life-sustaining fog.

Ferns carpet the dew-soaked ground

giving comfort to deep roots.

On this day I listen to whispers.

What wisdom do these trunks convey

as they stand  in natural wonder?

No worries about the future.

No anxiety about age.

A voice echoes in the depths of my soul,

*Precious things grow in the soil of time*

A faint smile crosses my lips.

I'm on holy ground in this sacred

sanctuary,  this Cathedral,

God's handiwork.

# A Day at Mercy General

*By Rebecca Johnson*

THE summer I was twenty years old, I volunteered at a local hospital. On this particular day I wasn't scheduled to be at the hospital. I decided to go to the local hamburger place. I was seated at an outdoor table not far from the street curb. I was about to take a bite when I heard screeching tires nearby, getting louder. I looked up and saw a fast approaching car coming toward the eatery. Forgetting the hamburger, I jumped up to get out of harm's way. The car was approaching so fast, it jumped the curb, barely missed the table but managed to stop. To my astonishment, I recognized the driver was my next door neighbor, Kenny. He bolted from the car and came toward me.

"Your father's in the hospital with acute appendicitis and has to have emergency surgery. Did you drive here or do you want me to take you to the hospital?"

"Oh Lord, yes I have my car here. Will you follow me there?" I cried.

"Of course."

We raced to the hospital, the very one where I volunteered. We got there as the doctor and nurse were prepping Dad for surgery. Kenny had to leave me and go to his job at an auto repair shop.

The operation lasted three hours. After surgery the doctor told Dad they wanted to keep him for five days for observation; Dad was taking antibiotics to treat an infection. On Dad's fourth day of recovery, on my scheduled volunteer day, a nurse asked me to help her take my father to another part of the hospital for some tests. When we got to his room there was a flurry of activity at his bed. The nurse told me to wait outside while she found out what was happening.

After many anxious moments, the nurse, with the doctor, came out of my father's room, gently took me by the arm and said, "We're very sorry, but your father has died."

"How is that possible? You said the operation went well. He was in recovery, getting stronger."

"His blood tests showed an infection. We were trying to manage it with medication. We don't know if the infection had spread or your father had a violent reaction to the medicine. We will find out what went wrong. We're so sorry."

"We've been trying to contact your mother; we haven't been able to reach her. Can you tell us where she is?"

"My parents divorced some years ago, and my mother travels a lot of the time," I told them.

"Well, she'll need to be notified."

"I'll try to contact her later," I replied.

"We need you to wait here; we have to document what transpired. We'll come back to get you," the doctor said.

Stunned, I collapsed in a sorry red chair in the hallway. What seemed only a little while later, the nurse reappeared and asked me to come with her. She helped me up and led me to my father's room. At the door, almost in a whisper, she told me she needed me to help her take my father down to the morgue; no one else, professionally speaking, was available to assist her and a witness was required to oversee the procedure.

When I entered the room, I saw the covered body, my father's body, already on the gurney. I blindly walked alongside the nurse as she wheeled the gurney to the freight elevator. My eyes drenched, I stared at the draped body on the way down to the morgue, unable to realize that was my father.

I could only think, *one day, this will be me, covered up, heading to a morgue.*

The morgue was cold and clinical, with a lone desk and chair situated near the entrance. On one wall there was a huge metal door, like a freezer door. I was frozen in a nightmare. At the desk, the nurse was filling out some forms. She opened the desk drawer and grabbed some keys. She turned the lock to open the metal door. She wheeled the gurney into the adjoining room.

The nurse came back out and said, "I'm really sorry you had to witness this. I'm so sorry for your loss."

We went back upstairs, carrying the forms. I left the hospital that day in a foggy daze.

Then I heard bells in the distance. "Oh, Church bells," I said to myself, "how appropriate," until I realized it was the alarm clock.

# D' Light

*By Wallace Watson*

In
My backyard
Shadows dance
In all directions

Turning this
Reality into dreams
Of a living
Paradox

A destroyer of hate
I am
A lover of joy
And happiness

Born of a fierce God
I am
The creator of
Delight, honor, and me

In another dimension
I evolve into a
Shared consciousness
With all things
My mother and father made me
Transformed me away
From God
Into me

Reflecting in the mirror
My mother's eyes look
Into my father's soul
And I remember

All his power
In a moment of asking
His forgiveness is infinite
Child of a fierce God

I grow from the
Shadows of my feelings
Where all of life
Is Light

# Meeting Pete Seeger

*By Marion Kahn*

IN my student days I was a great fan of the Weavers. I heard them at concerts and midnight hootenannies at Carnegie Hall. My admiration for Pete Seeger grew when he defied Joe McCarthy's infamous House Un-American Activities Committee, which chose to label him a Communist. When I met Sy, my future husband, I learned that in his camp-counselor days he had encountered the Seeger family. So, years later, it was natural that Pete Seeger would be our house guest when he came to perform at Beloit College where Sy taught. On a very rainy afternoon I met Pete at the Greyhound Bus depot. When I introduced myself and inquired about his bus ride from northern Wisconsin, he responded with a frown and these words: "The windshield wipers didn't keep time with each other!"

Like all of his concerts, the one that evening was magical. More than any performer I could think of – in those pre-rock and roll years – he engaged and enveloped his audience. His enthusiasm was infectious. When he invited you to sing with him, when he pointed his banjo at you, you joined obediently and joyfully in "Oleanna" and "Wimoweh" and "Kisses Sweeter than Wine." After the concert I carried his banjo home as reverently as if it were a Stradivarius.

The next morning, before he left, Pete brought his banjo downstairs to breakfast to give David, our very young son, a kitchen concert of whimsical Woody Guthrie children's songs. He made David giggle and gave his mother a memory to cherish.

# Sunset Mood

*By Georgeanna Holmes* ────────────────

Unhesitatingly

the sun moves down the sky.

Another day

peeled and discarded,

flung into the abyss

of forgetfulness.


What did I do today?

Zilch.

What did I accomplish?

Nada.


Soon it will be night.

I'll sit beside a moonlit pool,

tell myself sad stories,

yada, yada,

write a poem about love and loss,

lay the soul bare.


Will anybody care?

# Fruits and Fig Leaves

*By Georgeanna Holmes*

O great wonderful world
of immeasurable distances
pole to pole, yet shrinking
day by day, for the miracles
of science will not
be halted.

Would that your labs,
your vials, your Petri dishes,
could find a golden path
back to a simpler Eden,
sinless fruits and fig leaves,
free and blue-sky vaulted.

# Two Songs

*By Norma Kipp Avendano*

D ID you ever wonder what shaped your life? What drove or pulled you along? Did you think you were in charge? Did you think there was a plan or did life just happen by chance? Did you ever have a passion, a dream that lay in your heart? A dream to be nurtured … or put aside as improbable … just a nice thought … and you went on your way…? Can I apply these questions to myself?

I was just a poor little girl growing up in north Georgia who in 1937, at age ten, saw a movie with Gene Autry singing "Springtime in the Rockies" … so far away from Georgia.

*When it's springtime in the Rockies I'll be coming back to you,*

*little sweetheart of the mountains with your bonnie eyes of blue.*

*Once again I'll say I love you while the birds sing all the day*

*when it's springtime in the Rockies, in the Rockies far away.*

Composer Hank Snow

When I was twelve, I saw Gene Autry, again, in the movie called "South of the Border Down Mexico Way." He sang a song by the same name.

*South of the border down Mexico way,*

*that's where I fell in love where stars above came out to play.*

*And now as I wonder, my thoughts ever stray*

*south of the border down Mexico way.*
Composer Jimmy Kennedy and Michael Carr

Is it possible those songs shaped my life?

I grew up, still in Georgia, and at eighteen, I married a Marine who took me to Camp Pendleton, California near the north border of Mexico. There he took me to Mexico, south of the border, and I fell in love with its people, landscape, and culture. He loved it, too, and our home was filled with recordings of Mexican music, and we bought things from Mexico for our home. When he retired, we settled in San Diego where I began college to become a teacher. We planned, when my college years ended, to summer in a community near Guadalajara. Five years later, I finished college and began teaching a fourth grade class in a school near our home. One of the units I was asked to teach was "Living in Mexico." *Oh, Fate, you are so good to me!*

Within three months my husband was diagnosed with terminal cancer. We heard of a treatment in a cancer clinic in Tijuana that gave him relief and postponed his death three years. Was that the end of my love affair with Mexico? No, it was only put on hold.

In three years, I married a man with a Spanish surname who grew up in England. He had migrated to Toronto, Canada with his first wife and children. When that marriage ended, he came to San Diego and we married in 1968. His oldest son moved to Alberta, Canada, and my and Tony's many trips to the Rockies and Lake Louise began. They were the most beautiful places on earth to me.

Did *Springtime in the Rockies* replace *South of the Border Down Mexico Way?* No! In 1970, my daughter met and married a man from San Marcos, Jalisco, Mexico and went there to live. Sixteen months later, when time drew near for their baby to be born, Tony and I went to San Marcos to visit them. My daughter returned with us to San Diego for the birth of their baby, and when her husband obtained his green card, he came to join them and got a job in Los Angeles. When the baby was eighteen months old, they went to Mexico for a visit and left him there with his Mexican grandmother and aunt. Wanting and needing to have Carlitos in my life, Tony and I began visiting him twice a year in this small pueblo close to Guadalajara where Harry and I had planned to spend our summers. We had come full circle in regard to Mexico.

In July of 1975, I enrolled in a five-week program to study Spanish in Guadalajara, through the University of San Francisco, where I could live with a Mexican family. Tony and I drove there with the intention of leaving the car with me. Initially, I was assigned to the home of a young widow who had signed for seven students: five men and two women. When Tony and I arrived, the lady was not welcoming to us women. On the drive to San Marcos, 60 miles away from Guadalajara, to see my grandson, I decided to return to San Diego with Tony and forgo my plan to study Spanish. I was heartbroken. But when we returned to Guadalajara, and I went inside the house to get my luggage, the atmosphere was different. On the couch sat a Mexican nun who introduced herself in English. She extended an invitation from her parents across the street to have me live with them. My problem was solved. To my surprise, the name of the father of the family was Carlos Gallardo, the same as that of my grandson. And the name of the street was *Calle Misioneros.* Missionary Street. Tony flew home to San Diego, knowing I was in a welcoming place.

During those five weeks, *Señora* Gallardo smiled knowingly when I haunted the mail slot daily, and saw to it that the phone line was kept open on Wednesday and Sunday nights at the time Tony made his calls to me. When he returned five weeks later, *Señora* Gallardo and their entire extended family attended the *gran fiesta* María Jésus, Carlitos' aunt, had for his fourth birthday.

We returned at Christmas in our motor home to visit my grandson and the family in Guadalajara. The Gallardos thought we should sleep in their house while Pancho, their twenty-year-old son, slept in the motor home. While the matrimonial bedroom was being prepared for us, Tony and *Señor* Gallardo disappeared into his workshop where they opened a bottle of *tequila* and a little later emerged as *amigos.*

Our acquaintance ripened into a friendship that flourished and deepened through our numerous return visits and Gallardo visits to our home in San Diego. I attended family baptisms, weddings, anniversaries, confirmations, and birthdays in Guadalajara. My husband and other traveling companions were always welcomed in Guadalajara and San Marcos. Twice, a fellow teacher from my school and I went to wonderful Mexico City to see its sights before going to Guadalajara and San Marcos to spend time with my grandson. Another visit was Easter week 1978, when on Good Friday, an even dozen of us crowded into Roberto's Volkswagen van and toured the sights from noon until sunset. *Señora* Gallardo, whom I called *mi madre segunda,* my second mother, was in failing health, but she had rallied enough to accompany us that day.

She seemed especially joyful, and I put aside my concern for her health and asked when she would be visiting me in San Diego, an invitation I had frequently extended.

With wise and loving eyes, she looked deeply into mine, raised her right hand and measured a tiny space between her thumb and forefinger and said, *"Dios me està dando a mi solo un poquito mas de tiempo."* The translation was clear to me: God has given me only a little more time. Her face showed complete serenity and I thought, "She is ready to go, but can we accept her going with equal grace?"

I telephoned her six weeks later from San Diego on May 10, Mother's Day in Mexico, and read a simple greeting in Spanish from my prepared text. I was unable to understand her reply. Face-to-face we seldom had problems in understanding because we read each other's faces and eyes. Despite the language problem, I have been forever grateful for that call, because one month later, Pepita called from Guadalajara to tell me *mi madre segunda* had died in a diabetic coma following the amputation of her right leg. She had spoken of the anticipated surgery on Mother's Day, but I had not understood. That same week the flowering African violet, my Easter gift to her, apparently also died. Two months later when I was again in Guadalajara, Luz Maria sagaciously pointed out new growth on the wilted plant, which they had been reluctant to throw away. They all believed my coming brought the plant back to life!

I began teaching Mexican folk art when I retired from teaching in 1982; my collection is all over our home because I wanted to see it and use it. One year I went to lovely Oaxaca City to purchase clothing for the classes I was teaching and saw the pyramids Monte Alban and Mitla. In 1986, at the request of the Art Superintendent, I created three media kits with curriculum and activity guides on "Living in Mexico" for the school system in my hometown of La Fayette, Georgia and gave a great presentation. Imagine my joy in delivering the kits since I had first heard the song "South of the Border, down Mexico way" in 1939 with little expectation of ever going there.

When Tony retired, we traveled to the Yucatán Peninsula twice where I visited all the pyramids in the five states, as well as the museums and cathedrals. The precious visits to the pyramids gave me peak experiences and were soul-expanding as were the stops in magnificent Chichén-Itza, Isla Mujeres, Merida, Playa del Carmen, Cancún, Cozumel, Compeche, San Cristóbal de las Casas, Palenque, Villahermosa, and San Juan Chamula's famous church that requires special permission to enter at Easter when we were there.

On the western mainland there were visits to Matzatlán, Tepic, Zapopan, Tlaquepaque, Vera Cruz, Taxco, and Papantla where the Flying Indians gave us a personal performance on their forty-foot pole. We traveled many times on the Baja Peninsula to Bahia de Los Angeles; Loreto, home of the first of the Junípero Sera Missions; and La Paz. Once we went out in a small boat among the gray whales in Scammon's Lagoon near Guerrero Negro. In 1978, over the New Year, we were stranded for three days at El Rosario when the highway was flooded. From our motor home we accommodated many car dwellers for sleeping and meals and became known as the Itasca Cantina.

After Tony died in 2000, I took cruises to the Mexican Riviera. My book *On the Road with Members of the Family* chronicles our detailed visits to Mexico over the years, as well as those to the Canadian Rockies where we went not only in the springtime, but summer, autumn, and winter. On our last trip in 2000, I was able to film the full moon rising over beautiful Lake Louise at five a.m. in freezing temperature.

All the people I knew in San Marcos have died, even Carlitos who died in 2008 at age thirty-eight. He had been living with his dad in Los Angeles since 1984.

Two songs! "South of the Border, down Mexico Way" and "Springtime in the Rockies" … Would my life have been the same if I had never heard them? *Quien sabe?*

# Don't Do It To Yourself

*By Joe Torricelli*

You know I can't stand it when you

suck a butt

You want me to know you're ready

for the Adult World

Sure your body's young and tough

Wave the cancer stick with grace

Suck in a deep cloud of smoke

toughy, blow it into my face

What's one more puff,

puff,

puff

# Tee-Hee-Hee

*By Shelly Burdette-Taylor* _____

Sunday morning at Penasquitos Lutheran Church
Pastor preaches the sermon
In typical character – keeps the congregation entertained,
      laughing

My number one and only grandson Adonis, of 17 months, sits
      on my lap,
Waving to others coming into the sanctuary
Husband of 38 years, Tom, next to me
Mother, MeeMaw, 85, directly behind me

Congregation breaks into the first bout of laughter during the
      sermon
Adonis – sits up straight; completely still – looks around to see
      what's so funny

Once the congregation quiets down
Adonis starts to TEE-HEE-HEE loudly
He TEE-HEE-HEE's for so long
Must exit the sanctuary and go to nursery

# When Love Doesn't Heal

*By Katherine A. Porter*

This grandmother's love
nestled the boy safe among teddy bears
soothed away woes that never took root

He didn't notice his father's deep scars
his mother's raw sorrow

This grandmother's love
foresaw the child's fears
healed his wounds
harvested his loss
replanted them all
within her loving heart

He was not her child.

He is not her child.

He's back where he belongs
with his war-torn father
with his struggling mother

The boy is now raised
by what feels right to others

This grandmother has no rights
no more than a stranger
she lives clutched by fear
for the child she loves as her own

Can this grandmother's love heal?

# Intelligent Life

*By Bil Fuhrer*

*It started way back with a
     very big bang
or a pop and a fizz or a pow
     and a clang*

*But no one is sure just what
     happened that day
the universe started. It's just
     hard to say*

*Some scientists say that it
     came from a dot
that was too small to see but
     incredibly hot*

*That dot then expanded for
     billions of years
creating the planets and
     stars far and nears*

*All this from a dot? That is
     hard to believe
But why would our scientists
     try to deceive?*

*So I'll just accept what they
     tell me is true
which certainly makes me
     feel closer to you*

*And closer to flora and
     fauna and earth
and all of the cosmos that
     sprang from that birth*

*But something has
     happened, I'm sorry to
     say
that tantalized humans to go
     our own way*

*For as we evolved alongside
     of the rest
we started to think perhaps
     we were the best*

*We think and we reason, we
     grip with our hands
This gives us the power to
     rule all the lands*

*To kill all the animals, cut
     down the trees
To reshape the earth and to
     conquer the seas*

*To create a country where
     freedom is king
Where speaking your mind is
     a prevalent thing*

But some do not like this,
    this freedom of speech
They say that it violates all
    that they preach

So we need protection from
    those we despise
The ones who our leaders
    say threaten our lives

We start out with rifles and
    cannons and swords
But that's not enough to
    protect from war lords

So we build doomsday
    bombs that can kill
    everyone
Then drop one or two, just to
    show how it's done

Now many years later, we
    have a big mess
Our enemy's building this
    bomb with success

So we must build more
    bombs just so they can
    see
We're big and we're strong
    and intend to stay free

Then they must build more
    bombs to jump on ahead
And on goes the race till we
    all end up dead.

It's intelligent life that has
    brought us to this
Intelligent life that could
    cease to exist

It's intelligent life that I'm
    not too sure
Will ever be able to thrive
    and endure

We took evolution and
    rushed it along
In ways that looked right,
    but we may have been
    wrong

Our science is super, our
    medicine too
But without understanding
    we soon may be through

So picture this dot where the
    scientists say
We huddled together on
    opening day

Let's try to accept what they
    tell us is fact
And use it to guide us in how
    we should act

Toward humans and flora
    and fauna and earth
And all of the cosmos that
    sprang from that birth

# Virginity

*By Cheri LaLone*

I was nineteen with my virginity still intact, not that I didn't have many pursuers. At the age of eighteen Mom and I counted the boys I had dated at least once, twenty-nine in two years. We were impressed, considering I started dating in the middle of my sixteenth year and we weren't sure if we had remembered them all. I wish I could find that list. Just pondering this idea begs me to make another list of boys who impressed me enough to remember their names.

I loved boys, but the lingering fear of pregnancy was always present, and my orgasmic fever was fast and furious. Kissing, hugging, back rubs, lap humping always resulted in a roaming, startling sensation centering in and around my clitoris. This exploding force of ecstasy ran through my limbs to the tip of my toes, end of my fingers and out the top of my head. It was like a whole body yawn with a sugar attack of lust and wonder.

Climaxing: one of the simple pleasures of a young girl mixed with guilt and doubt. I never understood this duality but my Catholic education at St. Fred's did plunge me into altered states of pleasure, then sin. After the burst of pleasure there was no point in going any further. I would ask to be taken home and lucky me they always did.

Strangely enough riding a horse resulted in the same eruption of pleasure. I wondered if the girls who loved horses shared the same experience, and is this little pleasure also a sin. I bet that's why women rode sidesaddle. Bob Boatwright: I do remember him. We were in the back seat of his GTO when he called me a prick teaser. He was a beautiful bad boy, charming, with a body that would entice the devil. Maybe he was the devil. It was rumored he impregnated more than one girl.

So my advice is this: don't take off your clothes if you can climax with them on. Be satisfied, willing and proud to be called a prick tease, and remember you just saved this prick from being a teenage father.

# I Always Knew I Could Fly

*By Jene Alan* ─────────────────────

HIGH, HIGH IN THE SKY
I KNEW I WOULD
I THOUGHT I COULD
TAKE OFF ON A WHIM AND JUST BARELY SKIM
      ACROSS THE
LEAVES OF THE TREES, NEVER SCRAPING MY
      KNEES
FLY AWAY, FLY AWAY, FLY AWAY HOME!  LIKE A
      LADYBUG
LIKE A SWALLOW ON THE WIND, OR THE WIND
      DOWN THAT HOLLOW
FLY ABOVE, WAY ABOVE ALL THE DO'S AND
      DON'TS
ALL THE WILLS AND WON'TS
AND I DID AND I HAVE AND I WILL DO IT AGAIN
FEELING THE POWER, FEELING THE FLOW
I WILL AND I STILL GO AND GO

UP, UP, AND AWAY!
HELLO DOWN THERE, YOU STUCK ON EARTH FOLKS
HELLO DOWN THERE, YOU WILL OR YOU WON'T
      FOLKS
LOOK UP HERE.
               LOOK AT ME.
                         I CAN FLY!

# The Talk

*By Christopher Britton*

CHRIS picked up his phone, put it down again and stared at it. *I hate this.*

He picked it up again and dialed the familiar number; ears up and alert, he listened to it ring.

"Python residence, Paul sssspeaking."

"Paul, this is Chris. How are you?"

"I'm fine, Chrissss. How are you?"

"Me too. I'm fine too. Listen, can we get together sometime real soon? I need to talk to you."

"Sssure. I'm free tomorrow. Where do you want to meet?"

"There's a lion's kill that just opened up outside Nairobi a few days ago that I've been dying to try. How 'bout we meet there for lunch?"

"I don't think I've heard of it. What's it called?"

"The Wildebeest."

"That's a chain, isn't it? I tell you what, I just ate about a week ago, and I'm absssolutely ssstuffed. How about we jussst go for a ssslither down by the lake. If we go around ten, all the nocturnals will be in their dens, and we'll have the place to oursssselves."

"A slither … a walk … sure. That works. Ten o'clock is fine. I'll meet you down beside the marsh at the parking lot near the south end."

"Sssounds like a plan. Sssay, before you hang up, can you tell me what you want to talk about?"

"I don't mean to be mysterious, but I'd really rather wait until we're together, if you don't mind."

"Oh ... okay. Well, sssee you tomorrow at ten." Paul hung up.

Chris held his phone out at paw's length and heaved a deep sigh before putting it back in his pocket. *I hope this goes well.*

At ten after ten the following morning, Chris was pacing back and forth along the edge of the marsh. He glanced at his watch. *Where is he?*

"Chrisssss, it'ssss me. I'm down here."

"OH! Paul, you startled me."

"Sssorry. It's kind of what sssnakes do. Anyway, what's thisss all about?"

"Paul, we've been friends for a long time, right?"

"Yeah ... sure..."

"It's Bernice, Paul. She's asked me to have a talk with you, man to man, hyena to snake, you know ... like that."

"Why? Is sssomething bothering her?"

"As a matter of fact, yes. She says that the last few times you've been together, you've made her feel 'uncomfortable.' That was her word."

"Chrisss, I don't know whether Bernice has noticed, but sssnakes make everybody 'uncomfortable.'"

"No, there's more to it than that. She says she thinks you behaved 'inappropriately.' Again, her word, not mine."

Paul stopped in mid-slither and raised his head. "Inappropriate how?"

"Well, she says that a couple of times she's caught you looking up her skirt."

"Looking up her ssskirt! Where am I sssupposed to look for heaven's sake? She's eight feet tall. What am I, eight inches? When I'm with Bernice, there's nowhere to look but up."

"Paul, you're eighteen feet long."

"Right, but you don't sssee me toe dancing, do you? Eighteen feet long but with only eight inches of elevation. Besssides, have you noticed those ssskirts she's wearing these days – way too short for a girl her sssize. Why, she must weigh a ton."

"Two tons, actually. But that's not the point. If she's uncomfortable, something needs to be done. The two of you have been friends too long to let it fall apart."

The two friends resumed walking as Chris continued. "Plus, there's another thing. Bernice doesn't like the way you stick your tongue out at her. She says you're behaving like some kind of rock star, that it's overtly sexual, and that it's becoming 'pervasive.' Another one of her words."

"That'sss really hurtful. I mean, look at the sssize of Bernice's ears, then look at the sssize of mine. As ssself-absorbed as she is, she can't have failed to notice that I don't have any. That'sss why the tongue – to pick up vibrations, but, of course, it's all about Bernice. She'd never ssstop and think about sssomeone else's handicaps."

*Oh, great. I knew he'd get all defensive.* "Paul, all I know is Bernice thinks you're hot for her, and she just wants to stay friends."

"HOT FOR HER! MY G…"

"Paul, don't have a hissy fit…"

"Wait, did you just sssay what I think you sssaid?"

"…Oh, Paul, I'm sorry. I didn't mean … It's just an expression. I *am* sorry."

"Okay. Okay. I know you didn't mean anything by it. Forget it. It's just that this whole conversation is so frustrating for me. I mean, for Bernice to think sssuch things of me, when she and I have nothing whatsssoever in common."

"…Well … She thinks you're hot for her trunk. I mean, we've all heard of 'leg men' and 'tit men.' Bernice thinks you're a 'nose man.'"

"I'll give her that. She's got a GREAT nose, but she's ssstill not my type. I mean, those dust baths she takes, ugh. And have you noticed her ssskin? It has more lines on it than a topographic map. She really needs to have sssome work done."

"Paul, that's easy to say for those of you who can afford to molt. But you're still missing the point. It's not about 'types.' It's all about power. Throughout history guys have held power *vis a vis* women, and it's the exercise of that power guys get off on, not some hope of romance."

"No, Chrisss, you're missssing the point. Bernice's complaints are the kind of thing sssnakes get all the time. Always have. If there's one species that's been trampled by hissstory, it'ss ssnakes. Look at the Bible. Does Eve get blamed for the expulsion from Eden? Not hardly. It's poor old 'Vipero,' that's who. Moses casts down his ssstaff when he's talking to Pharaoh, what's it become? A sssserpent! 'Sssnake in the grass,' a derogatory term. The lissst goes on and on. Outcasts! Untouchables! We're the lawyers of the animal kingdom.

"Of course Bernice doesn't get it. How could she? She's an elephant. Babar, Dumbo, cute little comic creatures. Elephants are the media's darlings. I'm sssurprised Bambi wasn't an elephant!"

"Paul, don't go playing the species card with me. Hyenas haven't exactly fared well in the public's mind. I don't think we'll ever recover from *Lion King…*"

"Oh, boo hoo. Why don't you try being cold-blooded for a few months? Not ssso bad down here at the equator, but head north a few degrees – one sssnow flurry and it's all over. No sssuch thing as a ssskis sseason for sssnakes."

"Paul, don't make me laugh … Literally, don't make me laugh. We all have unattractive features, all of us. I can't even chuckle without everyone in a half mile radius staring at me. My wife has refused to go to cocktail parties with me for years.

"Bernice may be a princess, but she has issues of her own. For example, have you ever seen her dance? Not a pretty picture. She's got no self-confidence. Why do you think she always wears gray and tries to lose herself in that herd she hangs out with?

"Maybe she is demonizing perfectly innocent behavior on your part, but it's real in her mind. If you're truly her friend, you need to address it. The last thing you need is a sexual harassment complaint against you. I mean, look what happened to Bob Baboon just a couple of months ago. Why, there isn't a female primate in the entire Ngorongoro Crater he hasn't offended. Without some sense, some empathy for how your behavior makes others feel, not only are you asking for trouble, you're the lesser for it."

The two friends moved on without talking. The lapping of the water along the nearby shore was the only sound. Apart from the heat waves rising from the path ahead of them, they were the only things moving. Eventually they found themselves back at the parking lot. Paul turned to Chris.

"You know, I never thought of it that way before. You're right. I need to stop all this self-pity and reach out to others. 'If everyone lit just one little candle…' isn't that how the saying goes? You're a good friend, Chrisss, to both me and Bernice. Here, let me give you a hug before you take off."

*A hug?* Chris hesitated. "Thanks, Paul, but, if you don't mind, I'd really rather not."

# A Real Girl

*By Jene Alan*

Hey! I'm not just a good girl, a should girl, a would girl. I'm a
    jewel of a girl,

A cool girl, a sometimes do not follow the rule girl!

I'm not always coy-ous, joyous, ultra obsessed with boy-ous.

I'm a jewel of a girl, a cool girl, a sometimes do not follow the
    rule girl!

Sugar and spice, everything nice?

That's me and much more – I can tell you for sure

Body strength, endurance, brain power and assurance

Wiseness, trueness, authentic, not clueless

Savvy on Wall Street, independence can't be beat

Filled with gratitude, caring, kindness and sharing.

Cause remember

I'm not just a good girl.  I'm a jewel of a girl.

# Darkness

*By Dave Schmidt* ─────────────────────

Darkness returns, unwelcome intruder
How many nights to endure until gloom passes
Sleep, now welcomed, embracing darkness
Eventually the dawn, when light amasses

Deep sadness fills empty spaces
Will there be an end to this suffering
No relief in sight, holding onto distractions
Dark fantasies deepen the mourning

Mind lost in a maze of confusion
Will a time come to leave this state
There must be a way to end this delusion
No one else seems to possess this fate

Buried in a fleshy overcoat, a cross to bear
How long to endure the dark night of the Soul
Unseen but all seeing, surrounded by a torrent of activity
Aloneness and intense attraction, like a Black Hole

# Mother Rose

*By Elaine M. Fuller-Zachey*

My mother's life
is as this rose.
Its tiny bump, a leaf,
is being born
against receding icy snow.
It births freshness into the air;
I go to her.
Our restless sleep reflects
the coming of spring;
We are buds,
knowing that we will be
in the sun;
Whole, New, Free again.
We walk, Mother and I,
into her garden.
We sigh into its freshness,
away from confusion,
darkness, denial and pain.
We're here again
to try again;
Can we both unfurl, green and new?
Can we grasp the Beauty
of years together,
And this time not let it go?

# God's Gardener

*By Elaine M. Fuller-Zachey*

L AST night's thunderstorm pushed drenched trees over and one crashed on city power lines a block from us. Wind ripped through town, scattering limbs in streets and yards like garbage beneath their mournful, leafy parents. All this expression of God's fury mesmerized me, and I was amazed at how fast the city repair crew had arrived to saw away at the twisted body of the nearby giant tree. The crew quickly removed it from stretched wires without any lapse in electricity. Amazement flooded me as the voice of the repair crew's chain saw cut through the fresh, rain-washed night, its blade diving into the tree's center.

When I stepped into the early morning sunlight, I saw no evidence of the previous night's fallen tree, and then I joined my 80-year-old mother in the kitchen.

"There's trash all over – tree limbs and plants," Mom said. "I have to get out there fast and clean it up."

"I'll go with you."

She got up from the kitchen table, placed her empty coffee cup next to the sink, rinsed off her breakfast dishes and sat down in the chair near the back door. "It's wet out there. I'll need these." She pulled a pair of clear pink plastic rain boots over her worn down house slippers; then she stood, put Dad's big old tattered shirt on over her housedress and tied the ribbons of her broad-brimmed sun hat under her chin. "I'm going! Come out if you want."

"You and your gardening clothes!" I said and laughed. *You're the most beautiful person I have ever known,* I thought, *and you are really unique.*

"They're okay for me!" she smiled, went out the door and into the wet wild back yard.

As I cleared away my dishes, I thought of how Mom, a widow for many years, had remained so independent. Now she put more of her energy into gardening than even visiting friends and family. She loved to tell how a local newspaper had run a front page story with color pictures of her and the carefully tended flowers. Mom smiled brightly when she explained that people made it a point to drive by to see the eclectic but beautiful flowers in her front yard. Not only did my mother create a showpiece there, but she also half-filled the back yard with flowers and vegetables which grew in healthy green joy along the wire fence.

"This is amazing," I said as we walked around her back yard.

"Look at the roses," she sighed, pointing to pathetic twigs, petals and leaves that lay on the ground. Last night's violence had stripped flowers and leaves off her beloved plants, ripped off and straightened out curved vines and thrown them into mangled masses on glistening grass. "We have to get those," she said as she picked up one of the rakes. I took the second one. We began to rake drifts of leaves, twigs and larger branches into heaps. "We have to get this trash to the front," Mom said with a sigh.

"All right," I replied.

We stuffed leaves, sticks and branches into black trash bags as the morning's gray coolness dissolved into sunlight. I dropped two bags of trash beside the street in the front yard, then turned to go to the back yard.

---

Mom was walking toward me, dragging debris. *Here she comes, in one of her faded old dresses, Dad's old shirt that's too big and torn at the left front.* She stepped quickly, little feet encased in plastic rain boots, wearing her ancient hat. *Little, old, tough – how funny!* In spite of her age and odd appearance, she had the strong look and step of a determined, purposeful woman.

*She moves through this. It is all exactly, essentially Mom-gardener; strong-willed. Intelligent. Goal oriented. I have to memorize this ... keep it forever.* Time stopped. I stood there. I purposefully recorded my mother's walk, clothes and facial expression framed by fresh green plants and bright blue sky.

She smiled in the sunlight. "This is hard work!" She puffed as she tugged the garbage bag to its place next to the others.

"It sure is! Do you need to go inside for a little while?"

"No, not yet. It's almost done. Be sure you put one of those twistees on each bag. The garbage men won't take it if stuff spills out."

"Oh, yes. I did. I will."

Then my mother headed for the back yard and I called after her, "I'll be right there."

At that moment I realized Mom, as co-creator with God and caretaker in her yard, had the role of directing Nature into color and form that delighted everyone who saw it. She organized roses, shade trees, lilac trees, chrysanthemums, tomatoes, squash, cucumbers and berries into a living symphony. She planted, fertilized and pruned these lovingly, as though they were her own children.

*You are part of the Unity of Creation, a lover of plants and storms. You also love the Hand that sent the rain, wind and lightning. You, as part of this place, this time, this action, are essential in bringing it all together to form a specific pattern within God's Truth. You must have been there, Eden, and you missed it so much that you recreated it here.*

I watched, watched ... photographed her carefully with my mind – so she and this moment would forever remain a part of me.

Mom and I lived so far apart that frequent visits were impossible. As the years passed, her increasing dementia symptoms ended her visits to me so that I only visited her. Our phone conversations became almost impossible. I had to shout so she could hear and finally she understood only "How are you?" and "I love you."

My mother's long good-bye eased her more and more into her next life expression. It slowly removed her from me until the day I was with her in the hospital in Syracuse, New York, where she viewed her final sunrise from her window. As the dawn's soft glow bloomed, she crossed a bridge I couldn't see and was gone.

Although she is no longer with me, the mental picture of Mom as God's Gardener; the image's color, feel and Mom in it, as it thrills me now and always will. I know she now understands why I just stood their watching her carry that debris instead of running up to help. I will always carry God's Gardener brightly and lovingly in my heart.

# Transcended

*By Elaine M. Fuller-Zachey* ⎯⎯⎯⎯⎯⎯⎯⎯

If I reach for you,

will you allow me

to take your little hand

and lead you back,

if only for a moment?

There's so much to tell you;

days, years of my life.

You were so busy

with your long good-bye

part here, more and more there

until you saw your last earthly morning

through the hospital window.

Peach-colored and lovely,

the dawn gently kissed you

and you went on your way.

I did my best.

If it was too little,

forgive me.

# For the Bride, Ora Lee

*By Elaine M. Fuller-Zachey*

Serene, you wait
hands folded left over right,
gray hair sweetly curled
a touch of makeup.
Your wedding dress is cream
with peach flowers,
soft peach-colored jacket.
You meet your husband, my father,
Both of you attended by Jesus;
something borrowed–
my own cross of dark wood;
something blue–
the Lisianthius' deep blooms;
something old–
your wedding dress itself;
something new–
the casket, pink with pink roses;
Mother, I wish you joy
as you join my father
in your new home.

# Sorry

*By Rita Early* ————————————————

A tender caress

A slap in the face.


Sweet honeyed words fall from your lips

after the venomous bite.


Strong hands form a tight grip

around my neck.

# Walking the Dog

*By Shelly Burdette-Taylor*

Adonis with a new Amber puppy backpack
Bailey in a bra

Time to walk
In Marina del Rey

Adonis, 13 month old toddler
Wears his Amber puppy backpack
In Memory of Amber Basil Burdette Taylor
Golden girl, gift from God, pound puppy
Lived 13 full, fun years

Bailey, white fluffy poodle mix
Found on Highway 101, ears infected, hair matted
Leg dislocated, limping, weakly whining
Abandoned

Time to walk
In Marina del Rey

Bailey, now healthy and happy, skipping
Adonis struts his stuff
Proud to wear his Amber backpack

Each on a leash

# The Third Time
# I Performed CPR

*By Helen Antoniak*

PR – Cardiopulmonary Resuscitation – is the action taken in an emergency situation to restore the heartbeat and breathing of a fellow human being. I have taken CPR training too many times to count. I have performed CPR three times.

The first time was in June of 1967. I had driven with my parents from San Diego to the United States Naval Academy in Annapolis, Maryland. We were there to celebrate "June Week." The week's activities culminate with graduation at which the senior class of midshipmen is commissioned. My brother, Peter, was about to follow in my father's footsteps and become a Naval Officer.

We arrived Friday night and settled into our rented cottage. Early Saturday morning my father began experiencing severe chest pains and shortness of breath. I immediately began CPR while my mom called for an ambulance. I accompanied my father in the ambulance as it raced to the Naval Academy Infirmary. After further life-saving efforts were performed, the emergency room doctor pronounced my father dead.

I had not saved my father from death.

\* \* \*

I performed CPR again twenty years later in September, 1987. I was the founder, president and dean of my own university. It was a licensed, family, home daycare I called "The Baby University." I specialized in caring for babies from newborns until they walked. When the babies began to walk, they graduated – they got their "walking papers."

That fateful afternoon I went upstairs to find out why I had not heard baby Kevin awaken from his nap. I could not believe how he looked. I scooped up his little lifeless body. I called 911. I frantically performed CPR.

If I could have brought that baby back to life, I would have. Kevin would have been three months old the next day. "Sudden Infant Death Syndrome" is the diagnosis given when an otherwise healthy baby inexplicably dies in his sleep.

I was heartbroken about Kevin. That was the last day I cared for infants professionally.

\* \* \*

After I closed The Baby University, since I have a masters degree in social work, I found employment with the County of San Diego. The name of the department was Health and Human Services, and my job designation was "Children's Protective Services Worker."

Government bureaucracies are notorious for requiring paperwork, and social workers are responsible for completing the largest amount of it. After a decade of filling out forms by hand, I was expected to cross the digital divide. The County initiated a computerized record-keeping program called the "Child Welfare Services Case Management System."

Even though the trainers tried to gently ease us across the digital divide into a new, computerized way of doing things, I was extremely stressed. Until that historic transition, I had never even touched a computer. I had used many three ring binders in my life so having the computer training presented to me in a three ring binder was a good idea.

In an effort to calm my anxiety and master technological advancement, I created my own personal 'walking tutorial.' Before going into the office each morning, I would remove a page from the training manual, walk along the shore of Mission Bay and try to absorb the mystifying electronic procedures. I still remember how many steps were required where I was supposed to use the mouse and keyboard to select one thing and then click on another.

On a sunny morning in late October, I looked up from the page I was studying and realized I was alone except for a man lying face down approximately twenty feet ahead of me. I thought he might be taking a nap, but this seemed like a strange spot to choose. I would have been tremendously relieved if he were just sleeping, but I had to make sure.

"Sir, are you alright?" There was no response to my voice or the touch of my hand on his shoulder.

I knelt down and rolled the man onto his back. He appeared to have fallen on his face. I listened for his breathing and felt for his pulse. I could detect neither. There was no way for me to know how long he had been lying there, but his skin felt warm to my touch. I immediately began CPR. Soon a man approached me and I asked him if he knew CPR and he did not so I then asked him to get help.

After about ten minutes, a park employee arrived. He took over the chest compressions; I concentrated on filling the man's lungs with air. Paramedics arrived and sprang into action administering further lifesaving efforts with a defibrillator and an IV. They placed the man in their ambulance to transport him to a hospital. I chose to ride along because I felt it was important for the emergency room staff to know the circumstances in which I found the man.

At the hospital, I was escorted to a waiting room. After a few minutes, the paramedics came in and said I had done everything right. After a while, a doctor came in and also assured me that I had performed CPR correctly. The doctor then said that we had been unable to save the man.

Once more my life-saving efforts had failed, but this time it was a stranger. My mind would not rest. Who was this man? I wanted to know the name of the person I had tried to save.

Soon, a nurse came in and handed me a small piece of paper. I gazed with amazement at the letters printed on it. The man's name was "JESUS." I had tried to save Jesus. As a Christian, no name is more meaningful to me. I gave Jesus CPR. I bridged the gap between life and death with Jesus.

Because of the third time I performed CPR, I look at life and death differently. That earthly Jesus had made his transition into the arms of the heavenly Jesus for whom he had been named. I realize it was a gift from God to be present with my father and baby Kevin when their souls made their journeys to Jesus.

I know that someday I, too, will die. I do not know when, where, or how I will die. I may be alone; I may be surrounded by loved ones, or, perhaps, someone will be performing CPR on me. It does not really matter what the circumstances of my death will be because I will be making my transition into the heavenly arms of Jesus.

# My Daughter

*By Jeff Curtiss Welch*

LOOKING at her – secretly, appreciatively, unnoticed – I see my daughter as the last ditch effort of her parents to save their marriage. Tiny, vulnerable, even at 16. She never really had a chance – the deck being stacked against her before conception, before her DNA was set, before she "was." Her mother's strained face, my nervous twitches and darting eyes.

My daughter, the love of my life, created when I had none; a bundle of joy that brought none.

Memories like snapshots, no continuity. The baby became a girl becoming a woman when I blinked. Pages in a photo album, each one a multitude of missed opportunities.

Can others see the disappointments I have adorned upon her? Or can only the artist see what he ultimately created? Perhaps I simply dress her in my own failures, hang them on delicate shoulders that are still able to shrug off what she does not see in the mirror.

When her eyes meet mine, in the instant before recognition registers, she could be any number of young women looking up from a laptop computer. But that moment vanishes with the smile meant only for me.

Guilt drops from me like a shucked coat. The times I wasn't there are replaced with this time now. Her eyes pull me back through the years, beyond the broken promises she never made, to the only one she did.

# From Dreams

*By Dave Schmidt*

From early life to the present time
Dreams enhance, entertain our kind

From nocturnal stories, visions and nightmares
Dreams transport us beyond worldly affairs

From daytime fantasies and reverie
Dreams satisfy, illumine and offer escapes from reality

From beauty, excellence or amazing qualities
Dreams can epitomize our realities

From leading us forward with our goals
Dreams give purpose to our roles

From rich fantasies becoming the hero
Dreams may reinforce the hold of ego

From deep within and difficult to reach
Dreams await a time to teach

From experiences transient, confined to the mind
Dreams appear within to include our reality as defined

From all the dreams within our dreamy lifetime
Only the Soul, superconscious and sublime
*Daydreams ... Fantasies ... Stories*
*Nightmares ... Perceptions ... Goals*
*LIFE is a DREAM*

# Quarantine Creativity

*By Nancy Foley*

"CLANG clang" was the sound I heard as the authorities pounded the white metal sign into our front yard. In giant black letters, it read "Fourteen Day Quarantine." In the 1950's the Indiana State Board of Health required this procedure when a family member contracted a serious communicable disease. At seven years old I didn't understand the word "quarantine." However, I did know what "fourteen days" meant. As I gazed out of my window on that frosty February day, I realized that I would be in solitary confinement for a long time. I had scarlet fever.

We learned that this bacterial disease usually began with a sore throat, high fever, nausea and chills. A red rash would appear in the chest and neck area and spread throughout the entire body. Scarlet fever was considered highly contagious and, if not treated with penicillin, could result in life-threatening heart problems.

After my mother explained the seriousness of my illness, she told me that I wouldn't be able to play with friends or attend school for two weeks. To my seven-year-old mind, this seemed like an eternity. As my eyes welled up with tears, Mother also said that arrangements would be made for my older sister, Gretchen, and my younger brother, Michael, to stay with relatives. What I didn't expect was what came next.

The doctor spoke to me reciting his instructions like the harsh commands of a Gestapo General, "You won't be able to be in the same room with any of your family members. Your mother will be your only contact with the outside world.

All your toys and stuffed animals must be packed away in the closet. Any toys you play with during the next two weeks will be destroyed at the end of the quarantine."

I can still hear the door slam when my family left the room. I felt like I had been locked inside of a tomb. The silence was deafening.

The days were long. I passed the time listening to the radio, turning the round wooden dial to my favorite shows such as "My Friend Irma," "Fibber McGee and Molly," and "Queen for a Day."

I imagined what I would do if I were selected as queen for one entire day. My beaded white gown would be draped across the floor while my attendants showered me with gifts. There would be no silence as my subjects shouted "Long Live the Queen!"

If I had to be isolated, there couldn't have been a better place than the comforting haven of my royal bedroom. The wallpaper was a floral design, bouquets reflecting an eighteenth century English garden, perfect for a queen. My walnut, four-poster, spool bed had once belonged to my great-grandmother. Because of its regal height, a step-stool allowed my short seven-year-old legs to climb into bed. This was also a gentle reminder to kneel and recite my bedtime prayers. Against the north wall stood my antique walnut dresser with a secret drawer at the base where I hid all my childhood treasures. On the east side were two leaded-glass windows. I could lie in bed and view all the activity in the front yard and hear the excited voices of children, like soldiers, marching home from school. Despite the unpleasant circumstances of being confined and wishing I could join the fun outside, my bedroom felt like a palace: safe and secure.

When my mother opened the bedroom door, I couldn't see her beautiful smile because an imposing mask covered her face. She wore a stiff, white, sterile dress, and, at first, her presence startled me. Was she my mother or perhaps my royal nurse maid? She brought me meals, gave me sponge baths, changed my bed linens, propped my pillows, and endured the dreaded bedpan routine.

Looking back, I don't remember the physical pain from scarlet fever, but rather all the care and concern given to me. Since my siblings were gone, I had Mother's undivided attention. It wasn't long before I came to regard her as my guardian angel.

Although I didn't spend time with Dad during my illness, I eagerly awaited his arrival each evening. Like a "prince charming" he would stand outside my bedroom door making me guess what surprise he had for me. It might be a coloring book, a "Little Lulu" comic book, or another set of paper dolls.

My favorite was a paper doll family: parents, grandparents, three children and a dog. In my solitude, they became my subjects. I imagined picnics on the palace grounds and trips together to exotic lands. I also dressed up Jane Russell and Betty Grable paper dolls for trips to Sun Valley or Palm Beach, places where movie stars and royalty went on holidays. My imagination knew no bounds.

On Sunday mornings, I tuned the radio dial to Uncle Wally who read the newspaper comic strips. I pretended that he was my court jester bringing smiles and laughter to my palace walls.

At last, the two-week quarantine was over. I would be allowed to see my mother's face again, give my father a hug, and be reunited with my sister, my brother, and our dog,

Waggy. It's strange that I don't have a vivid memory of that glorious day when my health was restored. Instead, what I do remember is my mother's collecting and discarding all of the toys, books, and paper dolls that had traveled with me to many imaginary places. I felt a loss knowing that as I was rising with renewed life, these loyal friends were facing their final resting place in our incinerator. At that moment, the creativity that I had enjoyed in my royal palace disappeared as quickly as the quarantine sign was removed from the front yard.

# What's in a Name

*By Marion Kahn*

A recent L.A. Times column got me thinking about names. The Times headline was, "A young feminist surprises friends and colleagues by adding her husband's last name to her own." She quoted a friend who called this "a patriarchal tradition." In my day a girl wouldn't dream of keeping her maiden name – a quaint term, isn't it?

My maiden name was Belefant. Except for Uncle Charlie, ours was the only listing in the New York City telephone directory and I've never found one in another city. My father collected misspellings of our name. The list was long. Sometimes I wished for a name like Smith, familiar, easy to spell and pronounce, but mostly I liked Belefant. It seemed exotic. I enjoyed the mystery of a Romanian heritage which I knew virtually nothing about. In the '30s, when I was growing up in what should have been the rich cultural mix of New York, everyone was very busy being "American" and denying their heritage. It was a time of disdain for everything ethnic.

Still, I enjoyed living in fantasy land. All I knew was that my father's parents came from Jassy in Moldavia in Northeastern Romania. To me they were gypsies, colorful, dark, romantic wanderers. When I was a child, for Halloween I wore purple and red and turquoise skirts and fringed scarves and gaudy bangle jewelry – with my long dark hair and dark eyes, a very authentic gypsy, I believed. Now, many years later, I still wear purple and red and turquoise and have done my share of wandering.

When I visited Romania – on a Cambridge Art History tour during the Ceaucescu era when one could visit Romania only as part of a tour – I told myself that I felt at home as I continued to take liberties with our very sketchy family history. I remember a magical visit to the tiny Sibiel village church known for icons painted on glass. The women of the village, dressed in white blouses with fine black embroidery, began to sing "Mária, Mária." To me, absurdly, they were celebrating my grandmother for whom I was named, and who may never have set foot in a church.

My real Grandma Mária – accent on the first syllable – died a year before I was born. According to my mother, they named me Marion because people would mispronounce Mária, i.e., it was not American. I asked, "Why Marion with an 'o'?"

My mother replied, "Because that's the correct spelling." Thereby closing the subject.

Hardly a week goes by that I don't get a letter addressed to *Mr*. Marion Kahn. Even Viagra ads.

My mother's family had stories about names as well. So many people my age are children of first generation Americans who straddled two worlds, unsure of where they belonged or who they were. Names seemed to symbolize this shaky identity. They were often changed, "Americanized," by their owners or by others. It would be decades before the concept of multi-culturalism was invented or valued. Richard Rodriguez writes about the American dilemma of identity and what he calls the necessary betrayal of one's heritage.

My mother, Flora Jasper – an acceptable name, one would think, bestowed upon her by her English mother – was renamed Florence by her elementary school teacher. The teacher simply announced, "Flora's not a real name." And Florence she remained for the rest of her life.

Last names were changed as well, sometimes as an arbitrary act by immigration officials, but more often to disguise their ethnic origins in order to "pass" in an Anglo-Saxon society. By the later 1940s, with the glut of World War II veterans applying to universities, especially to medical schools, aided by the G.I. Bill, there were quotas on the number of "non-Anglo" admissions. I remember application forms that actually asked, "What was your name before it was changed?"

While millions of Jews were being killed in gas chambers, and during the years immediately after the war, a sensitivity, even a paranoia, existed among American Jews. Perhaps this was especially true, though unspoken, in young people trying to shape identities and at the same time sensing some troubling message that to be Jewish is to be inferior or unacceptable. When we were teenagers, my friend Rhoda Shapiro used to introduce herself as Ronnie Sanders.

I wonder if I grew up without uneasiness about my name because Belefant is not an identifiably ethnic name. I delighted in the fact that my favorite French teacher called me Mademoiselle Belle Enfant.

What's in a name, indeed!

# Go For It

*By Jene Alan*

*Forget mistakes, forget failures, forget everything, except*
*what you're going to do now and do it. Today is your lucky*
*day.* Will Durant, *Story of a Civilization*


You could, you have to, you won't need to try
To make mistakes, a pile, high as the sky.

Mistakes are important, mistakes are a sign
You're on the right path, a path that's just fine.

When you learn a new skill, like playing ball,
Mistakes are the steps toward knowing it all.

Mistakes say you're trying things not tried before,
And you're not going to quit till you've tried much, much
more.

Mistakes are just puzzle pieces for you to work through
To earn a new ribbon, the color of blue.

Mistakes are necessary, more than okay.
They're the journey we take to create a new way.

Is it okay to make mistakes? Well, it just better be!
'Cause everyone makes 'em, all of us ... one zillion and three.

Mistakes are not failures, and shouldn't be hid
From your mother, your father, or any new kid.

They are badges of courage!
You're taking a chance,
Walking your talk,
Learning to dance.

# La Matinana

*By Joe Torricelli*

Come see Dawn in her white
Dress, as she lifts the cover of
night. She comes with the Sun
in the morning making the
whole world bright.

Life sparkles with dew drops, bugs
scatter the light of day. Tiny lives
buzz, hum, bid us wake. Make love in
their small world, the Garden, find
joy in another new way.

Darling put on your flimsy see-
through. Let me see you as you really
are. Love's life at its beginning,
breathing your honeyed breath.
Smothered in heady desire let me love
you again and again.

# In Motion

*By Dave Schmidt* _____

In Motion all things around us unceasing
observing the play and display of creation

While stranded on a rock revolving and
orbiting endlessly around a hot, gaseous cloud

With a world full of animate objects that
arise, grow and become recycled

With nature governed by a time
that can be viewed as relentless

In a Universe that is continually unfolding
without properly knowing its ending

Observed by a restless mind that is
striving to make life more meaningful

Based on an ego that is constantly evolving
with our deepest fear in the self for losing

All the while doing nothing and going nowhere
the inner silent witness of Self consciousness.

# The DMV

*By Joe Torricelli*

If you drive an automobile from
point A to point B
There's a pot-hole you can't miss
it's called the DMV
From the dawn's early light you'll be
tested – the vehicle code, the road test,
the eye chart, oh say can you see?

Stressed-out DMV checker how do you
think I got here?  Steering with one
eye on Vehicle Code, or was it the will to
survive?
Regarding your threatening invitation,
Dispense with your testing. I don't need
another senseless death-defying ride.  If
I'm on your list of the tax-paying public,
I most certainly can drive.

# Why I Write Poetry

*By Lloyd Hill* ————————————————

Because my mother read me nursery rhymes.

Because in school I wrote notes to girlfriends.

Because I'm afraid of dying.

Because it will live after I die.

Because it connects me to my poetic ancestors.

Because I will influence future poets.

Because there will always be poets.

Because it makes me mysterious to myself.

Because it attracts women.

Because it needs solitude.

Because it forces me into crowds.

Because it fulfills every moment.

Because everything relates to poetry.

Because poetry informs everything.

Because I like the sound of church bells.

Because of it I must notice everything.

Because it makes details important.

Because it gives life meaning.

Because it makes tap water special.

Because it makes old folks sexy.

Because it makes me appreciate graffiti.

Because I have no formal religion.

Because I don't need to cuss so much.

Because it softens and hardens as needed.

Because it lets me speak in tongues to everyone.

Because I can write about wrongs in the world.
Because everything is subject to poetry.
Because every drop of rain is hope for the thirsty.
Because it helps those recovering from war.
Because it allows me to lead a minimal life.
Because it makes me happy.
Because I can be anywhere and enjoy it.
Because it continually reminds me I will die.
Because it fills my dreams.
Because it makes me feel different.
Because it helps me fit in.
Because it makes life worth living.          .
Because I have to.

# Where Do Babies Come From

*By Cheri LaLone*

MARYANNE was our neighbor and baby sitter. She lived with foster parents in a large brownstone on the corner of Franklin Blvd. and Henry Clay. She came to live with them when she was eight, an easy age to submit to duty.

It was a difficult life for her. If she was loved by the Hamilton's, I can't really say. She was the caregiver for their disabled child Eric. When I met Eric he was 12 years old, confined to a wheelchair or bed, unable to communicate with words or care for himself in any way. They shared a love and appreciation for each other that was based on survival. They were separate from the rest of the family: odd to live in a house but not be part of the home.

Time with Maryanne was always eventful, filled with stories of woo and games of trickery. Thoughts that made you think. There was a question and answer game. Her questions were always just beyond our comprehension. I was seven years old; it was 1955 when life was simple and seven-year-olds were innocent. The question Maryanne asked was, "Where do babies come from?"

With the certainty that Tuesday follows Monday I said, "When someone in your family dies and is buried, you wait for a few months, go back to the grave site and dig up your baby."

Maryanne laughed out loud.

"Cheri is that really where babies come from?"

"Ya, I think so.

"Well, what happens next?"

"There's a big party."

"Tell me about the Party."

I go into my private space in my mind, where my other family lives. Where magic and wonder are created. It's safe here.

It's a spring day; the flowers are blooming. The air is cool, the ground no longer hard; it welcomes a shovel. The mood is happy, there's music all around. The ceremony begins. Everyone has a large spoon, they all take turns; the ground gives way to a hole with a bubble. We step in for a closer look and ponder the wonder of it all. You can see the baby. Everyone joins hands praises God in a song for the gift this child will be.

The priest kneels, his ceremonial gown flows back with the wind. Everyone changes their position to watch him pull the bubble from the ground. He picks it up and says a prayer of welcome. He hands the bubble over to the doctor. Now time is critical. The baby is in a fragile state. The expected baby is placed in a delivery box that is clear with a warmed inner liner. The doctor and expected parents leave together, priest and family follow. When arriving at the delivery place, doctor, baby, mom and dad are in a separate room.

We are ushered into a waiting room; it's a light comforting blue with a circle of chairs. The smaller children sit in the center on the floor. There's not a lot of talking, Grandma brings up the possible options for the name of baby to be. This breaks the silence and calms the fears.

What happens behind the closed door, I'm not sure. I expect the bubble is broken. Mom breathes air into the baby's lungs and washes him up. The baby cries itself to a rosy pink color and is dressed in a baptismal gown.

The waiting family is anticipating the new mom and dad to walk out. The air gets tense as the time drags on. When the door opens, everyone jumps up and a song of celebration starts; this continues in a parade of hugs and kisses. A new life begins for everyone.

I look up. Maryanne and my siblings are wide-eyed and speechless. The children clap in a cheerful refrain but Maryanne says, "Cheri, isn't your mother pregnant?"

"Ya, but she's always pregnant."

My answer to the question where do babies come from made perfect sense to me. At the age of seven, reincarnation was a word and concept I had never heard. Today it is something I hang my hat on. It answers the question that there is a fair God, a second chance, a new beginning, a new opportunity.

# Paradise Ridge Vineyards

*By Michele Garb*

Leaving the mundane, I drive into paradise

After many years observing the land's progress

Parched, native brush and rock transformed into verdant,
　　　　fruitful vines

Even in the cool of the morning, picking season is always hot,
　　　　hot, hot


Perfectly formed, tightly packed grape clusters, plucked off
　　　　the vine

We pause occasionally, tasting astonishing varietal differences

Riesling, Cabernet, Zinfandel, Petit Syrah, Sauvignon Blanc,
　　　　Sangiovese

Buckets of heavy liquid-laden fruit dragged up to the cool,
　　　　lush lawn


Then a midday potluck, feast for the senses

We taste and enjoy flavorful unique dishes

Sampling last year's wine, savoring, comparing, and
　　　　contrasting

We chat and catch up with old friends, in our day of paradise

Shaded and surrounded by happy vegetation, the processing
       continues
Washing, crushing, pressing, and storing the soon to be
       fermenting juice
Bottling, corking, and labeling last year's wine creations
All concurrently worked by an army of friends our hosts have
       assembled

Later, processing equipment is washed, goodbyes expressed
Our hosts lovingly thanked
Leaving without wine, not possible
Under the host's eagle eye, no one departs empty-handed

Back in the car, thinking about paradise
Feeling like I've spent the day in a Tuscan vineyard
The trip home is much shorter
That night, satiated with fun, visions of the day float by, as
       sleep descends

# Take Me

*By Avery Kerr*

---

LMOST-five-year-old James McKay stood next to his mother as she put on her makeup. She pulled the low bench forward toward the mirror. "Powder puff, p-p-p-please." She extended her hand, palm open. Giggling at their game, James reached for the soft cloth circle, then watched as she smoothed her face into velvety perfection.

"La-la-la lipstick," she sang, before pursing her lips into an exaggerated pout.

On tiptoe, James peered across the array of jars, bottles and little boxes until he found the golden tube. He uncapped the cylinder, twirled the luscious red upward, and handed it to his mother. He watched her full lips bloom into a thousand roses.

Turning her head to one side, then the other, she admired her hair. "This was my grandmother's vanity."

"Dina..." Brent entered in a rush. "What time will your sister be here?"

"You look pretty, Mommy," James said.

Dina dabbed perfume on her wrists. "Thank you, my sweet boy." She glanced up at her husband. "Around five."

Brent checked his watch. "Friday traffic might hold her up. Let's call a taxi and meet Betty and Tom on time, for once."

"James-y." Dina pointed to the bed. "Please hand me my evening bag."

The boy found the satin clutch, and ran his hands over the rhinestones that glittered like real jewels. Dina snapped open the gold closure, extracted a quarter from her wallet, and handed it to James. "Scoot." Giving him a gentle nudge toward the door, she patted his bottom. "Tell your sister to let you watch *Bonanza*." As soon as he left, she frowned. "You know I don't like to leave the kids without a sitter."

"They'll be safe for half an hour." Brent handed Dina her coat. "Ellen's old enough and plenty bossy to keep her little brothers in line." He gestured toward the window. "Besides, it's snowing like a son-of-a-gun. We'll be grounded if we don't shake a leg."

Mr. and Mrs. Brent McKay needed this weekend off. Juggling the care of three children: Ellen, 11; Peter, 9; and James, the "surprise", was eating a hole in their marriage. Last week, when Brent had suggested the trip, Dina shook her head. "Leave them for two nights?"

"Tom's my boss; he expects us to socialize."

"But James' birthday is Sunday," Dina protested.

"We'll bring him presents."

"From the casino?"

"1962 Piper Cherokee."

"What's that?" She shrugged.

"Brand new plane. Never get another chance like this." Brent rotated his hips. "Come on, baby..."

Dina had to smile.

As Brent gyrated, he hummed, "...let's do the Twist."

When she laughed, he knew she would go.

Because she didn't want to smear her lipstick, Dina McKay air-kissed each of her children. The older two gave their parents half-hearted waves and went back to watching Pa Cartwright teach Little Joe how to shoe a pony. James grabbed his mother's legs. "No-no-no," he cried. "Take me."

Dina hesitated for a moment. She bent slightly, as if to pick him up.

"Taxi's here." Brent pulled at his youngest son. "You're a big boy now, James." He knelt so they were eye to eye. "Be good for Aunt Sarah. Mommy and I will be back for your birthday."

On Sunday evening, anticipating the promised presents, James waited in the living room. Around midnight, he curled up on the couch. Sarah covered him with a blanket, and waited for the door to open, or the phone to ring. The call came just before dawn. The plane had gone down near Tahoe. No survivors. Later they learned the pilot's wife, fearing the storm, had deplaned moments before take-off. James knew his dad would not have left the plane. Even if Brent had been afraid, he wouldn't show it. No, he'd hold Dina's hand, tell his boss a funny story, laugh off the blizzard.

Aunt Sarah, their guardian, insisted the kids call her "Mom." James said it to her face, but never with meaning. She became an expert manipulator, using their parents' death to coerce good behavior; pretending to know when Dina and Brent would or would not approve. Ellen's prom dress was "cut too low." Peter's friends were "not our type." Sarah explained to James that being a "surprise" baby wasn't necessarily such a good thing. She allowed him to drill a hole in the quarter, and bought him a chain so he could wear the talisman around his neck. Whenever she spanked him, James would grab the quarter hard.

During high school James kept the coin in his pocket. Several times a day he would check to make sure it was there by rubbing his fingers along the edge, and over the President's face. By the time he graduated from college, the token was so smooth and worn that he couldn't make out the year. Every major decision relied on a toss of the holy quarter. *Mommy and Daddy: heads; everybody else: tails.* Should he move to a bigger city? *No.* What about grad school? *Sure.* When he didn't get in, he asked again. *Guess not.*

His brother and sister weren't attached to their parents' belongings, so when James moved out on his own, he took what was left of their furniture, including the vanity. It looked out of place in his bachelor apartment. The mirror had grown cloudy, and the seat's plush upholstery showed threadbare patches. Although he kept a few lipsticks and several compacts, he couldn't identify his mother's scent. Was she wearing *Joy* that night, or *Youth Dew*? He remembered the rustle-y feel of her full taffeta skirt, and the click of high heels. He wondered how she'd made it to the cab through the thick snow. Valuing fashion above practicality or comfort, Dina hadn't worn galoshes.

Each birthday brings James pain. Powder puff, lipstick, quarter. The images cycle, building momentum, then dissolve into emptiness. When he turns thirty five, surpassing his father in age, James visits the site. A two-room wooden structure sits high on the side of the mountain.

"Once the lift's finished..." the proprietor points to empty racks and shelves. "...ski and boot rentals."

James nods, and follows him through a narrow doorway.

"Café'll be here." The space contains formica tables and some mismatched chairs. "Have some hot chocolate." The man hands James a packet of powder along with a cup and plastic stir stick. "Hot water's in the kettle."

Looking out the window, James squints, trying to find the exact spot.

"Enjoy the view." His host lifts a hammer from his tool belt. "Gotta get back to work. Hard to find help up here in winter time."

Sitting at one of the little tables, James sips the sugary mixture and stares at the mountain. He focuses on a particular snow-covered boulder and wonders if there's anything left. A square inch of wing, maybe, or a stray bolt from the engine. Perhaps a bead from her hand bag. He puts the quarter on the table and traces the familiar circle with his index finger.

Dina scoops him into her arms and tucks him into her coat. Dad, in too much of a hurry to stop her, opens the door. They bolt for the cab, which is idling in the driveway. On the way to the air field the windshield wipers can barely keep up with the wet snow.

The Piper Cherokee lifts and dips in the wind. The flask of brandy spills. Brent grabs Dina's hand and stares straight ahead. She buries her face in his neck so she doesn't see the mountain. Her ruby lipstick and dripping black mascara leave grotesque markings, like bloodstains, on his overcoat. James is sitting on his mother's lap, burrowing into the folds of her best dress, when she dies. He looks into Dad's blue eyes, and smiles.

He's a small freckle-faced boy, who likes Legos, and won't be starting kindergarten.

He's four. Forever.

# Fear of Wind

*By Nita Blair*

GROWING up in the Southeast I knew wind as a fearful, fierce, and destructive force, especially when in the form of a hurricane. Of all the wind storms, hurricanes are, by far, the most difficult to endure. They last for many hours of not knowing if you will survive.

I was five when I first learned to fear the wind. Daddy and I were living in Ocala, Florida with my stepmother and her family in a large two story-house on several acres of farmland and a large orange grove. Our home, constructed on tall pillars, was high enough for me to walk under the house without bending over, though I had to duck my head a bit to avoid large floor beams. During hot summer days, temperatures stayed fairly comfortable beneath the house, and frequent rains did not interrupt my activities. This became my favorite place.

One day I sensed an ominous darkening and then noticed large black clouds quickly forming on the horizon. Soon they covered the entire sky; day seemed to turn into night. Uneasy, I entered the house and immediately sensed tension in the adult's conversation as they sat in the living room. Southern children hear enough hurricane stories around the dinner table to acquire a deep-seated anxiety of having to face this violent monster that even adults seem to fear. My apprehension escalated. Upon hearing the frightening word "hurricane," my concern over the dark sky changed to a dreadful fear of the unknown.

Where to go? Where to hide? I pestered everyone until someone suggested the safest location to weather this storm might be under the house. Probably a ploy to get me out of the way; nevertheless, it was a suggestion I found comforting. After all, "under the house," my private place, my retreat, my playhouse, was where I always felt safe.

I hid under the house for what seemed to be hours and listened to the adults laughing and talking above my head. I have no recollection of what became of the threatening storm. Obviously it skirted our small town; however I still harbor a clear memory of that frightening afternoon.

Seven years later, while living in New Orleans with my paternal grandmother, hurricane threats, tropical storms, or just strong winds were frequent. No sirens, radio news or bulletins offered advance warnings or information. Grandma was our weather predictor; I thought she could read the sky. Sometimes she pointed to distant clouds and said, "See, it's raining over there." She could even smell rain before it arrived.

Usually we were either on the outer edge of a hurricane, or most of its power was lost by the time it reached us. Still I knew what it was to awaken in the night and feel our one-story, drafty house shake and rattle from the force of strong winds. I would snuggle closer to Grandma for safety before drifting back into a troubled slumber.

One hot, humid afternoon when a sudden thirty-degree drop in temperature made seventy degrees seem cold, dark menacing clouds called attention to a storm developing in the southeast.

"Could be a hurricane brewing," Grandma predicted.

That terrible night is still emblazoned in my memory as the epitome of what a hurricane is all about. A sleepless night

– the most frightening I have known. Would the next gust be the one to carry us off into a whirling unknown? During the wee hours of the morning, when most can usually drift off for a few winks, the hurricane reached its peak. I steeled myself to not jump in response to the next clap of unending thunder. Once in a while, when a bolt of lightning illuminated the room, a glimpse of the clock proved time had passed ever so slowly. Grandma and I pretended to be asleep, each hiding our anxiety. We were alone in what was widely known as the "second oldest house" in the suburb of Lakeview.

The fierce wind contoured man and nature's handiwork to its own liking. It never ceased its relentless flow. I almost learned to enjoy the violent caress of sustaining winds between the dreaded gusts. During these destructive lulls we could hear the clang of metal, the clunk of wood, the unnatural thrashing and snapping of tree branches, or a loud, explosive pop – the sound of a large tree trunk breaking.

Was the metal a piece of our garage's tin roof? Was the clunk of wood a part of our house or perhaps our neighbor's? I heard the fierce swishing noise of the china berry's boughs, then the sudden crack of another broken branch. Would my favorite climbing tree be there tomorrow? We burrowed deeper into the feather mattress in total darkness and listened for the approach of the next explosive force that could be our doom.

As the next blast of air approached, the roar built to an unimaginable crescendo of violent noise drowning out, as though inconsequential, the comparatively small sounds of breaking trees and dismantling structures. Only the thunderous roar of wind could be heard. Waiting for the destructive blast of wind to hit was a study in mental torture. Each second the sound became louder, until finally, the whole house seemed to explode in a shock of brute force. The creaks, rattles, and rumblings of wood and metal as the structure struggled to withstand another assault were second only to the brutal, shaking vibrations of the house and the occupants' nerves.

Like a dentist's drill, when the noise and grinding stop, the small pain left is almost pleasant; so it was with the wind. When the blasting gust passed, the continuing forceful damaging winds felt almost mild. Taut muscles relaxed a bit before preparing for the next onslaught. Hour after hour, I prayed for the storm's end to be near. Hour after hour, I hoped the next forceful gust would be diminished.

All of a sudden, quiet! Not a sound can be heard. Is it over? Nothing moves. Dead calm. Muscles and nerves slowly relax. For a few minutes we experienced a blessed relief of the deepest silence imaginable. Has it ended or, are we in the middle of the storm with the hurricane's eye over us? In the distance, the roar of an approaching gust begins from the opposite direction. Structures weakened from the first half of the hurricane are now pushed and pummeled on an opposite side. Now we suffer a repeat of the past hours of dark, roaring, tumultuous buffeting. Our terror continued from dusk to dawn.

Daylight broke into a beautiful sunny morning as if nature was pretending nothing happened. Quietly, almost in slow motion, neighbors began to exit their damaged houses to survey the debris and clutter.

Soon we discovered our "second oldest house in Lakeview," had become the oldest house. The previous holder of that claim, a two-story structure one block south of us, lay in matchstick rubble. Two blocks north of our home a fairly new house had been lifted off its foundation and placed intact, neatly, but backwards, on an empty lot next door.

Once again life continues. We were mere mortals surviving another of Mother Nature's tantrums.

# In Celebration of Your Life

*By Norma Kipp Avendano*

A version of the following letter to my son, who died in January, 2005 is found in my book entitled *Charles Eric Kipp, In Celebration of your Life,* published in 2013. It was read at his memorial service.

My dear Charles,

As my one and only son, you have been a precious presence in my life since you made our family complete on October 14, 1949. Now you have gone to be with your dad and I know it was a glad reunion. Here on earth, along with my sorrow, my heart is flooded with memories of you beginning with your birth when, in the arms of the assisting nurse, you scowled down at me, crying like a little warrior. My little warrior. Your scowl turned to smiles and even gleeful laughter during those nightly romps before your ten PM feedings when your dad, holding you high in the air with arms extended, 'dive-bombed' you around and around, up and down, swooping you toward me. On Halloween as a one-year old you laughed yourself silly at your sister Anne's devil mask when we thought you'd be afraid. At 17 months you said your first sentence at bedtime to your dad, "I'm going nighty-night, good-bye." Then at three, in a heavy downpour you informed me that someone had forgotten to turn off the water. And after every hug, you'd say, "Mommy, I love you all the much in the world."

I remember the ruined Thanksgiving when you were four and claimed the live turkey for a pet and wouldn't eat a bite when we cooked it for our dinner. You had such a tender heart. At the Grand Canyon you said, "I bet I'd be twelve years old before I hit bottom if I fell off this ledge." And you were only five. At six you dragged home a used Christmas tree for next year so we wouldn't have to buy one. Once, after taking too long to come home from school and I was upset, you explained that you had taken the long cut home.

Of my million memories of you, these come to mind today: your happy face when we came for you after a week at summer camp; your shaved head on the football team and we called you Mr. Clean; your playing with your dog, Buck, and your trying on your dad's Marine Corps dress blues. I remember when you played your guitar on the stage in Nashville at the State Convention in 1967 as a senior in high school, and when you graduated from UNLV in 1978 with honors in Philosophy. I remember when you brought Lauri to meet us at Christmas 1978 before your wedding in March on Long Island, New York, at which you had "California Here I Come" as your recessional, and when you handed one-week old Pamela to me in January 1986.

As a grown man you warmed my heart by saying, "One thing I am truly grateful for in life, and I'm sure has benefited me more than I am even consciously aware, is the 'spark of life' that both you and Dad always preserved, which you yet preserve, in life. So many let it die, or kill it, within themselves. I am so fortunate to have such a genetic inheritance as I do."

I praise your accomplishments in astrology that resulted in your book *Astrology, Aliester, & Aeon* along with mentoring others, me included, in its study. I know all that brought you fulfillment as did your poetry and philosophical writings in your search for TRUTH. But fathering Pamela brought you the ultimate happiness, as well it should because she is a fine young lady.

I hold close to my heart your expressions of love for me in person, by phone, in letters, and in the flysheet of your book where you wrote, "Much of its contents and style are directly attributable to your beneficent influence. The writing of it helped me to evolve toward our glad reunion. Love always, past, present, and future. Your son, Charles."

My wise, brave warrior, you faced life and death with courage and joy and that gives me joy and courage too. The world is a better place for your having being here.

Goodbye, Sweet Prince. May flights of angels speed thee to thy rest. I love you all the much in the world.

Mom.

# Lessons from the Wave

*By Erika Toraya*

THERE are waves that have the power to slide right under my board and pull me into the ride with effortless ease. It's a fulfilling excitement. Fluid movement of my body with the aliveness of the water underneath and a sense of accomplishment keep me going back for more.

Other waves look promising and seemingly build in height as they come closer, but once the wave reaches me, it reveals its falsity. There is not enough power for me to catch it. The wave keeps rolling, leaving me behind like a piece of dead seaweed. No matter how hard I may paddle or how badly I want it, exhausted and frustrated, I must let the wave go. I appreciate that not every opportunity is for the taking and life's path is greater than any one success. There is always another wave, or opportunity in life, on its way.

The tide, current, and swell of the ocean change things up each time I surf and remind me of the ocean's vastness and grandeur. It is in control, not me. The pace and power of the wave are unknown at first entry, but warming up to its pattern, I can acclimate and work with it.

There have been a few times when my friends and I decide not to go in because the conditions are not ideal. Watching from the shore, it's a decision to save time and body heat. Not every time will be a great surf day, and it's okay to skip. But then there are occasions when the waves are small and I overhear surfers decide not to waste the time. They are there daily and for me, it may be once a month. This encourages me to take the plunge and take it for what it is.

I am determined to get in the water and end up having a blast. The misjudged waves embrace me with joy and love. My determination pays off and those guys missed out! Small wave days can be some of the best surf sessions. There are fewer surfers, I have lower expectations, and the conditions are surprisingly better than they had appeared. Just like life, my attitude can be open to enjoying the opportunity and hidden adventure.

Then, there is the decision factor. Which waves to paddle for and commit to? It's not possible to catch them all. I wouldn't have the energy and it's not good etiquette to nearby surfers not to share. When the wave that is headed for me has good form, with enough power and in my space of safety from running into others, it's a gift I accept. It's time to put the power in the paddle and the will to achieve.

My confidence can be tested when another surfer may also appear to want the wave. He will be quick to take it from me if I hesitate so I must commit and believe. If I can catch it while he is still paddling, then it's my right-of-way and hopefully he will honor my position, see my determination, and move to let me go. The wave meets me, I grab on, and we are one. My spirit soars like the seagulls and dances with the dolphins.

It does happen when the occasional surfer knowingly snakes my wave, cutting me off and taking off with the prize. And other times when another surfer and I are both in position and he maneuvers in such a manner that prevents anyone from riding the wave with him. These are disheartening inter-actions. Maybe he does this because I'm a girl, but mostly because he's a jerk. But then, there are those who have let me go for and catch a wave when they could have also gone for it. Maybe he does this because I'm a girl, or just because he is kind. Either way, I appreciate it and feel the 'aloha' in the air. Like the moments when drivers or grocery shoppers let me in line or someone smiles at me while walking by. It fills me with appreciation. To enjoy the exhilaration and share goodness is what life and the waves are about.

There have been plenty of waves which I have let go for the surfer behind me because it's his right-of-way. He looks as if he's taking the wave. Is he going or not? *I could ride this wave if you just decide!* He takes a paddle or two but then doesn't commit and let's it go. Now it's too late for me to catch a good wave. What a bummer. But, better to have respected him and not be so concerned for my own gain. Plus, I know the feeling and appreciate when others are patient with me. I'm not a perfect surfer, employee, girlfriend or friend and it reminds me to keep things light. And what do you know, a few minutes later, a reward wave comes right for me!

The waves humble, empower, and refresh me. I let go of lost waves, root on others on their waves, and look forward to my next wave. When I strive to enjoy and share the great waves of life, there is peace. I am grateful for the ocean of life lessons.

# James Frederick Parker, Jr.
# 1945-1969

*By Susie Parker*

Sandy's eyelids flutter.

She turns her head on the tear-soaked pillow.

Someone standing there.

The light behind haloes the shape.

It's Jim!

Thank God!

The Civil Air Patrol has been searching the foothills for days.

He speaks,

"I'm sorry, Sandy. I couldn't make it over the waves."

Then he's gone.

Sandy rises, her right side soaking wet.

Jean enters the bedroom.

"What's wrong?"

"I saw him! I saw Jim!"

Fishermen off Oceanside find the wheel of a plane.

Nothing more.

Jim is still out there.

Sandy had been away on a flight. She was working for Western Airlines. When she got home, Jim's car was there, but not Jim. No note, just an empty bottle of rum on the counter.

When the phone rang, it was her sister-in-law, Jean, inviting them over for a family dinner at the apartment she had near Cal State Fullerton. Explaining that she was waiting to hear from Jim, Sandy declined the invitation.

Hours passed. Jim did not call. Sandy wondered what he could be doing. Again, the phone rang. It was an official at the Fullerton Municipal Airport where Jim was getting his pilot's license. The person on the phone said that a Cessna was missing and that Vance's car was there. Vance was Jim's flight instructor. Jim and Vance were last seen having a drink at the airport bar. Now the plane was gone, and so were they. No flight plan had been filed. The Civil Air Patrol was conducting a search of areas near Fullerton, desert and foothills.

Sobbing, Sandy called Jean. "I'll be right over." Jean replied.

They hovered by the phone, pacing the apartment, drinking tea, holding Kleenexes to catch their tears. Jean suggested Sandy lie down for a bit. That's when Jim appeared to her.

Shaken, Sandy relayed the vision to Jean. They did not know what to make of it. There was a puddle of water on the floor near the bed.

As they were puzzling over what had just happened, another call came in. It was someone from the Civil Air Patrol. They had been notified that a wheel of a Cessna was found offshore, near Oceanside.

Jean called the family with the disheartening news. Mom had gone to bed. When told of her son's disappearance, she was still in bed, unable to face the grief she knew was there. Dad, shaken, fighting tears, readied for the drive down to the Coast Guard Station. The wheel needed to be identified. He called Sandy and Jean to let them know he was going. They insisted on going with him.

Down the 5, past San Onofre, past Camp Pendleton. Dad could only stare ahead, preparing for dealing with a piece of the evidence of what had gone wrong. Sandy sat in front, arm draped over the seat, holding Jean's hand. No one spoke. No one cried. It was all wrong. This could not really be happening. Not to Jimmy, our son, brother, husband.

He had always gotten away with daring behavior. When he was two, he jumped off a Navy pier, next to a battleship. A sailor dove in and found him, pulled him up. He was perfectly calm and smiling. No fear. When he was four, he fell out of a two story window, landing on the lawn. Again, no injuries, no problem. He seemed to have a charmed life.

He did cause grief for our parents from time to time. He did not take anything seriously, especially school. Dad, a poor farm boy from Mississippi, had worked his way through Georgia Tech. After graduation, he had joined the Navy, gotten into flight school, earned his wings in Pensacola. Now he worked for North American Aviation, the Apollo program. He still flew on weekends using private planes for family vacations and adventures.

One weekend Dad took Jimmy and me out over the ocean near Newport Beach. There we did "power dives." Dad pointed the nose of the plane straight up. We climbed and climbed. The engine would stall and we'd be a free fall until Dad could restart it. It was thrilling.

Once, playing with a Ouija board, Jimmy asked it, "When will I die?" His sisters all groaned and protested, "Jimmy! You're not supposed to ask stuff like that. Ask about getting married or something." The pointer went to the number 2 and then to number 4. Jimmy asked another question. "Where will I die?" Again, all of us protested this scary line of questions. The pointer went to O C E A N. We tried to convince him it was silly, but then he told us of his psychic experience in Hong Kong.

While in the Navy, he had leave in Hong Kong. He went to a psychic with some shipmates. They all asked about the faithfulness of girls back home. Jimmy asked about his death. He was told "You will die in a plane crash in the ocean when you are 24."

He had never told anyone that story before. Our family has a strong belief in psychics because one had predicted the meeting and marriage of our mom's parents in 1919

Jimmy had turned 24 that August, had married Sandy in November. It was December 9, and he was missing.

At the Coast Guard station, Dad showed his retired Navy ID and they were directed to the hangar that held the wheel. Once there, Dad collected it. Sandy and Jean could not hold back their sobs. They were barely able to walk back to the car. They sat huddled together in the back seat and wept as Dad grimly drove back to the Fullerton Municipal Airport.

He had to get the wheel to their lab for analysis, to see if the paint matched the paint of the missing Cessna. He could do no more, no less. Taking Sandy and Jean back to the empty apartment, Dad hugged them. He told them that at least now they would know something.

His heart was breaking, but he would not give in to his grief in front of Sandy. He could not burden her with that.

Driving home, Dad could barely see the road as the tears came. He knew to pull over. After some minutes of private weeping, heart aching, stomach turning, Dad got back on the road and went home to face Jimmy's mother, his own beloved wife.

Many years later, I went to a psychic referred by friends. I was thinking of changing my career, and wanted some spiritual guidance. I made an appointment, drove to his home. He greeted me at the door. He seemed very ordinary. No turban, no flowing pants.

He showed me to his basement, where he did his readings. We sat in chairs. He closed his eyes and concentrated. "I'm getting a message from the Beyond! Do you know a Helen or an Ellen?" I told him I had a cousin named Helen. "The message is for her to lose weight or she'll have heart problems." I was shocked.

I got to ask about my career choices next. "You'll be teaching art in a private school."

Then I asked about Jimmy. We had never found him.

"There will be a major earthquake. The plane is lodged in an underwater cave. It will come loose, float to the surface." Thanking and paying him, I went home to ponder what he had said. My cousin had always been overweight. She was also sweet and kind. Would it hurt her feelings if I advised her to lose weight? I decided I had to.

I called Helen, and, after catching up on family news, told her of my reading with my friends' psychic. She was quite surprised and then told me something astonishing. She had just gotten home from the ER when I called. She had gone in with heart palpitations. The doctors had told her that she must lose weight.

I never did get a job teaching art in a private school.

There have been plenty of earthquakes.

Jimmy is still out there.

# Again

*By David S. Larson*

FLOORBOARDS shake as heavy feet work to stomp out the cold. A metal latch scrapes and a door squeaks open. Two anxious yellow dogs push aside a middle-aged man and nuzzle into me, their noses cold and wet with excitement. I'm not afraid.

The man looks up and down the quiet country lane and turns back. "Let's see what we got here," are the first words I hear Earl Harris say. He plucks me from a small wooden box off his front porch. The year is 1902 and Earl is my first father.

I grow up Rachel Harris in the heart of rural Connecticut tobacco fields and Yankees who never stray more than twenty miles from home. Earl names me after his mother who came from England in the mid 1800s. Earl never marries. Instead, he chisels gravestones, mostly from finely peppered New Hampshire granite. His hands are large and rough but not his manner. Not a day passes where his kind words and the echoes of iron-on-stone do not follow me.

On a wet spring day when I am seventeen and off at school, a wall of marble topples over and crushes Earl. They said nothing would have saved him, but I think I could have done something.

It takes me two weeks to carve his marker and he would have been proud. "Etched in our hearts forever. Earl Harris. 1861-1919." I see him six months later – after I catch influenza and die.

\* \* \*

One last touch from her – a gentle kiss – then she sets me down and disappears. A tired Model-A groans to a stop on an empty dirt road and concerned hands lift me up. It is 1931 and they name me Elizabeth, now the youngest of their five children. Even in the oppressive heat, Dorothy Langston clutches me tight. She smells of Boraxo and lemons. She is my first mother.

Though only twenty-nine, my mother looks fifty. Her once lush body has collapsed under life's unfair burden of too many mouths to feed and an angry husband. Henry Langston had worked a small ranch in southern Texas until locusts took his feed and his cattle starved. He settles our family in a small New Mexico border town where he scratches out a living doing odd jobs. By my fourteenth birthday, he has already raped me thirty times.

"You ain't kin to me anyways," are the last words he spits at me. I leave home that night unaware I am pregnant. With money stolen from my mother's coffee tin, I come to Los Angeles. At a bus terminal, alone and not knowing what to do, I meet Gary Willis, a soldier returning home to Montana. I go with him and become his wife.

After ten years of marriage and four beautiful children, Gary opens a small hardware store. We live in a modest house he builds with the help of friends. Then, following two years of invasive tests and a final decree, I take my last six months to say goodbye to my children and my husband. I am laid to rest, a victim of unknowing medicine.

* * *

I see her face this time. At least I think I do. She makes one final tuck of a pale blue blanket to ward off a crisp, fall

Minnesota day – and she is gone. Rebecca, a Sister of Clemency, finds me by a back door. "Not another, not another," she wails as she carries me through the vestibule into the Mother Superior's chambers. They lay me on a table and remove my clothes. They search for deformities and other signs of the devil. I am baptized Evelyn Grace. It is 1961, and now I have many mothers.

The orphanage stands alone overlooking the slow, dark Mississippi River. Every weekend during my first two years, eager couples look me over – then turn away. The other children begin to taunt me and I fall inward. By my fifth birthday, I hardly speak, but thoughts explode in my head.

When I turn seven, the Clarkes take pity on me and bring me into their Jehovah's Witness home. Under their care and home-schooling, I begin to unfold. Two years later we move to Wisconsin where they adopt Raymond, my five-year old brother. We feel like a family should – and it feels good.

On an icy winter day when I am fifteen, my mother drives me to buy my first bra. The police report estimates she is going only thirty miles an hour when our car careens into an oncoming truck. She is killed instantly. The doctors are prepared to give me a transfusion and remove my leg, but my family's religion doesn't allow it. I reunite with my mother later that day.

\* \* \*

A bright mist teases the quiet morning air. Small pebbles give way under cautious feet as I sway beneath a pendulum of care. A heavy door opens to the smells of a warm hearth. My eyes try to focus.

And then – her voice. It coos. It sings. It runs to me and tickles my nose. It fills my lungs.

She picks me up and holds me close and says the only words that will ever matter, "I'll never leave you … again."

# We Stand

*By Erika Toraya* ————————————

We stand and pray
Together we share
Our hope, the despair

How can this be
Why do they choose
An option in which we all lose

If she only knew
If he could hear the facts
Peace, love, answers they lack

Moments of calm
Accepting this mission
It's a battlefield we live in

Other times
Feeling of desperation
"Please see your child as a real creation"

Hear the choices
Other voices
Real love above the noises

Mother leads daughter
Refuses information
Misguidance in this nation

Isolating mother controls the situation
A father accepts the devastation
Be parents of protection, inspiration

Hurts my heart all too familiar
Family of isolation
Child needs personal affection

Standing on the sidewalk
A chasm between life and death
Drastic decision takes my very breath

We should all object
Clinic saying life imperfect
Lies, danger for money they can get

A situation to inspect
Our world's despair and disconnect
Fears cause us to reject

This child, alive and well
For easier life, will be forsaken
Becomes a piece of trash collection

The white truck arrives
For baby parts, forgotten lives
Pray them to heaven, goodbye

We stand and pray
Together we share
Hope, despair

Together let's stand
This is all man's land

# Be My Valentine

*By Rita Early*

---

I T was the night before our first Valentine's Day together. I wondered what Chris had planned. He hadn't said a word, and while I didn't want to ruin any surprise he may have lined up, I needed to know what to wear for the occasion.

"Hey, tomorrow's Valentine's Day," I said as if the thought had just crossed my mind.

He barely turned from the TV. "Yeah, I'm so glad we don't care about Valentine's Day. It's just another Hallmark holiday to get people to buy stuff."

"Who says I don't care about Valentine's?"

"You mean you want flowers and candy sent to you just because some corporation says we should?"

"When have you *ever* bought me flowers?"

Silence.

"Just let me know what you want me to tell my colleagues when they ask me what I got for Valentine's Day. Should I say you were too cheap or that you don't love me as much as their boyfriends love them?"

"Oh," was all he managed to say.

On Valentine's Day I got a dozen red roses and a gift basket with bath salts, soaps and lotions. Within a week the flowers died and a year later, I still had most of the bath salts. The soap and lotion got used up by house guests. *Obviously, I need to be more specific about what I want.*

"Honey, remember the flowers you got me last year for Valentine's Day?"

"Yeah."

---

"Well, they died and that was kind of depressing. How about you get me a plant this year instead? It will last a lot longer than flowers and every time I see it I'll think of you. Oh, and for dinner, I want to go to Ruth's Chris Steak House."

"Sounds like a good idea. But, in regards to the plant, if you really want it to last you longer how about I just get you some seeds?"

"Don't deviate from the plan. I don't like surprises."

# Honoring Adonis

*By Shelly Burdette-Taylor*

Adonis
Greek God of beauty and desire,
A twelve-year old Honduran boy

Born with a hole in his heart
Short of breath, anxious, on oxygen
Barely speaks

Dane, on a mission in Honduras, 2009
Making rounds with the nurses' in a pediatric ward
Prays, conducts healing touch and gentle massage

Meets the family of Adonis
Bonds immediately
Dwells with the family
Bringing the hope of Jesus

Adonis comfortable, quietly breathing
Sleeping, smiling
Life saving heart surgery
Remains a dream

In memory of that twelve-year old boy
Who died in May 2009 in Honduras
Dane names his son Adonis, born May 2012

# Mixed Up

*By Rebecca Johnson* _____

Wake up to a sparkling blue sky morning
But soon dark clouds sneak up
I want to pull up the covers again
Hole up, wait until it brightens up
I lie awake thinking up ways to pass the time

Clean up the kitchen, heat up the soup
Straighten up the living room
Sew up a hole in my sock
Curl up with my cat
Catch up on some reading
Finish a poem, write up a story outline
Make up songs to sing

Call up my friend Clyde, find out what's up with him
Perhaps he'll come for a visit, when the rain lets up
We'll walk up the street to the park, hike up the hill
Soak up the view, wait until sunset
Eat up a picnic supper
Lie on the grass, gaze at the stars
Doze off in the cool night air
Dream up what we'll do tomorrow

# Cut Me Some Slack

*By Jim Crakes*

Now I've been told I'm getting old
And need to see a doctor.
That's not the way God made this mold
So don't get me a proctor.

The get up and go, my tour de force,
Has been sitting around more often.
Some of my skills have diminished, of course,
But don't hurry me to the coffin.

The spring in my step is not quite as brisk,
And I'm slow with crossword puzzling.
But to step off the curb is still not a risk;
My wife says she still likes my nuzzling.

My hair has gone white a little too soon
And skin on my arms paper-thin.
The knees when I walk play a funny tune
Accompanied by pain in the shin.

Don't sell me short you cocky young males.
Don't offer your seat while I stand.
Some wind may have gone out of my sails,
But I can still play in your band.

# Do You Remember?

*By Robert McLoughlin* ────────────────

Do you remember when it was quite okay
For us to be young at heart and also to be gay

When fag was a cigarette and grass was to be mowed
When pot was just for cooking and wild oats to be sowed

When web site was a spider's flimsy space abode
When punk lighted cherry bombs and ethics was the code

And rock was just a big stone and stoned was what you got
When you slept with enemies, not when you were a sot

And buns were the hot-cross kind, a boob a stupid oaf
And bread wasn't money, we ate it by the loaf

Of course there was another thing that we all quickly learned
You never sat upon your butt, or else you would get burned

And when you gave your girl the bird it was always in a cage
But when she gets the bird today she flies into a rage

And chip was just potato or buffalo back then
And now a chip is silicon and that's beyond my ken

Mary Jane was my girlfriend and not a name for pot
And weed was just an icky plant that grew out in the lot

And sex was the difference 'tween Mary Jane and me
And not something that we did, we called that a spree

And fix was something very bad you got yourself into
And now it's also something bad that somehow gets in you

Cross-dresser was a stylish girl and boy could she be mean
Today it's neither boy nor girl but something in between

A dyke was pliers in a box of tools and toys
Not a girl that slept with girls in preference to boys

Bitchen's what your parents did if you didn't do your chore
Today it is a word of praise for someone you adore

Mooning was my feeling for that new girl at the dance
Not a pervert on the bridge taking down his pants

Pissed was baby's diaper, a job for Mom or Dad
Now it is your state of mind when you are really mad

In olden times when we were cool we put on more attire
We snuggled with our honeys and started up a fire

Streaking was the sun's rays streaming through a cloud
Not the antics of some nude running through a crowd

Hanging out today is a folksy social scene
Not a fatty at the beach looking quite obscene

Scarf you wore around your neck on a cold and windy day
Now we call it scarfing as we pack the grub away

Switch-hitter was a ball player who batted either way
Now it's a bisexual who swings from straight to gay

On almost all these modern words I'd like to cause a pox
With just one small exception, that is called a fox

It used to be an animal with bushy tail that curled
But now it is a creature that's the best one in the world

I'll gladly swap those oyster shells if I may keep one pearl
The name that I like best of all, in other words - a girl

# Choices

## By Frank Primiano

THE creature would not cooperate. Every time it landed on the damp sand, its eight legs churned. In no time it had burrowed beneath the surface. So, as soon as David found one and put it aside to look for another, the first would disappear.

Minutes before, David had discovered the first sand crab of his short, three-and-a-half-year life. He had been startled and not a little scared by the small, wriggling, bug-like thing that had appeared in the shovelful of sand from the hole he was digging. But curiosity had taken over. He spent some time examining it, not noticing the incessant waves that erased the depression he had created.

If David had been about 15 years older and in a college biology class, he might have learned that the one-and-a-half-inch-long North American sand crab is indigenous to saltwater beaches along the Atlantic seaboard. And that the female lays eggs in the shifting tides, then abandons her tiny offspring even before they hatch days later. For their part, the baby crabs are armed only with their instincts to burrow in the wet sand to search for food and to save themselves from their enemies: the ubiquitous gulls and sandpipers, the crushing tires on the lifeguards' patrol jeeps, and, now, the explorations of a little boy.

But none of this was David's concern. He had made a wondrous discovery and wanted to tell the world. Balancing a tiny crab on his shovel, a grin bisecting his face, he ran the twenty-five yards from the edge of the surf up to the dry, low dune where Bo lay on a blanket. Almost out of breath, more from excitement than from the run, David announced with pride, not caring who heard, "Daddy, Daddy. Look. I got a cweachah on my shubble."

Bo sat up. He shaded his eyes with one hand and steadied the toy shovel with the other. The crab was in its death throes as the sun's rays drove the moisture from its body. Never having seen such a "cweachah" before, Bo recoiled at first, betraying a caution and distrust of the unfamiliar born of years on the street. But after a probing finger escaped serious injury, he decided that this little beast probably wouldn't do anyone much harm.

David was beaming with pride. Bo smiled. "It's a neat little bugger, ain't it, Davey? Where'd you get it?"

"Down der in da sand," David said, turning to point toward the spot where his excavation had been. "Can I keep it? Can I keep it in da van wid us?"

"I don't know ... maybe," Bo said, pausing to reflect. "We'll see... For now, why don't you go back down there and try to find some more?"

"Okay." Delighted, David scampered off, repeating, "Cweachahs, cweachahs..." Again he was careful to keep the crab on his shovel as he ran, almost stumbling in the soft footing.

\* \* \*

Bo watched a happy David return to his digging just within earshot of the blanket. Now sitting up, Bo lit a cigarette and surveyed the nearly empty beach. The sun had begun to drop from the sky behind him. The air was losing its warmth as it did at this time of day, at this time of year. In about an hour the beach patrol would drive by and chase the last stragglers home. You could count on it – like clockwork.

Bo's thoughts returned to what he had been pondering when David had startled him with his cweachah.

*Life's been a bitch lately ... ever since I got fired. It's not fair. I didn't miss that many days. And now unemployment's run out. Man, what a rut. And this habit ain't helping me get another job. Shit, I need money to get high, and for food, and to buy gas so's I can go look for work, or make a score.*

*That ad on TV says,* "A person shouldn't have to choose between healthcare for his children and putting food on the table." *Well, I gotta choose between putting food on the table for the kid and getting a fix.*

*It was after Haley went and died that things started goin' to hell. What did I get for spending three years with her? Hooked on coke, and a kid to take care of. And he ain't even my kid. She was schleppin' him around when I met her. Damn, she didn't even know who the father was. So she OD's, and now I got a schleppee.*

The cigarette he was smoking had almost reached the filter. He buried the butt in the sand and lit a new one.

*It's a good thing I hooked up with Cheryl, or me and Davey wouldn't even have made it these last few months. But, anymore, she's always spaced. Hell, we come down here for a last look at the ocean, a last day at the beach, and she's sacked out in the van. Even so, I can't get along without her. I just wish she got along better with the kid. I guess I can't have everything.*

*It should be easier in Atlanta. Ed and Janie said I can find work there and we can stay with them until I get set up. At*

---

*least it won't be as bad as around here, especially with the cold coming on.*

*I hope we have enough scratch for gas to get there ... and for a couple of dime bags to hold me and Cheryl over 'til we can tap Ed for some dough. Things'll work out ... they have to.*

*Anyway, I'm glad I could bring Davey to the beach one last time before leaving. The kid always seems to have fun here.*

\* \* \*

David's interest in his cweachahs was waning. The breeze had a chill to it now as the sun found the western horizon. The last of the crabs had burrowed away and David didn't bother finding any more. He was getting hungry. He stood, and, with his shovel dangling from his hand, shuffled toward the blanket.

It wasn't until he had walked almost twenty yards that he realized that he couldn't see the blanket, or Bo, up ahead. He looked back to where he had come from. No blanket in that direction either. He turned completely around. Nothing ... nobody. The beach was deserted.

Tears welled in his eyes just before he let out a mournful wail at the top of his lungs, "Daddy ... Daddy..."

There was no answer, only the repetitious roar of the waves. He began to cry. He cried until he was gasping for breath and his knees grew weak. He dropped onto his bottom and sat whimpering, wearing himself out. At last he lay down on the still-warm sand, curled up, stuck a salty thumb in his mouth, and fell asleep – the deep, exhausted sleep of the innocent. Not even the pesky sand fleas made him stir.

*　*　*

When the baby sand crab is abandoned by its parent and must fend for itself on the shore, it hides in the damp sand, protected from the seagulls, the sandpipers, and the tires of the life guards' vehicles. But lying on the sand, unprotected, David couldn't avoid the attention of the gulls that circled overhead in the fading light, looking for one last chance to fill their gullets. They landed, and, emboldened by hunger, came closer and closer.

David also couldn't avoid the headlights of the beach patrol attracted by all those ravenous birds that surrounded a small, motionless creature holding onto its little shubble.

# Author Biographies

**J**ENE Alan
She loved music, hiking, ping pong, and books. As well as ice cream and chocolate, to which she soon lost her looks. She laughed till she cried. She lived till she... She loved and was much loved in return. "Here she comes!" said Mom and Dad. And there she goes!

**H**ELEN Antoniak
Helen grew up close to the Point Loma Assembly where the Writers Workshop meets. She retired from a social work career employed by the County of San Diego in Health and Human Services. Helen enjoys writing, walking on the beach, taking pictures and hearing what her classmates have written.

**N**ORMA Kipp Avendano
Norma settled in San Diego when her husband Lt. Colonel Harry Kipp retired from the Marine Corps. He died in 1965. In 1968, Norma married Tony Camilo Avendano. She retired from teaching in 1982. They traveled widely before Tony died in 2000. Norma enjoys associating with friends, traveling, writing, and painting watercolors and gourds.

**K**. J. Baird
Once an academician and a wetland scientist, K.J. Baird is new to the world of creative writing and storytelling. "F243" is a nonfictional account, colored with imagination, of a recent DMV trip. She hopes you find the story as enjoyable to read as it was to write.

NITA Blair
Born and raised in New Orleans, LA, Nita moved to San Diego in 1951. She worked ten years as a secretary at Convair and General Dynamics. While living in Mission Beach, she met and married Jim Blair. They have two sons and six grandchildren. Nita has attended the Writer's Workshop for almost a decade.

CHRISTOPHER Britton
Christopher is a retired lawyer, former Marine and enthusiastic cyclist. He has written a variety of novels, short stories and poetry, mostly for an audience consisting of his desk. He, his desk, and his wife, Nancy, live in Serra Mesa.

SHELLY R. Burdette-Taylor
Dr. Burdette-Taylor is nurse, educator, writer, wife of Tom, mother of four adult children and one precious grandson, Adonis. Shelly is a US Army Nurse Instructor and small business owner of TayLORD Health, LLC. She and her son, Dane are missionaries in San Pedro Sula, Honduras conducting nursing education and holistic health care.

TIM Calaway
Already a world traveler by the age of ten. Tim now resides in San Diego. He brings his varied experiences to life in his poems and stories of lost loves, lost dreams, and lost fortunes.

# MARY Carnes

Mary retired 14 years ago from federal service, is a wife of 29 years, mother to three sons, stepmother to two daughters, grandmother to 14, and great-grandmother to five bonus great-grandsons. She's glad to be back in the writing class after an absence of four years and hopes to complete Memoir #2.

# JIM Crakes

Jim was born and grew up in Eugene, Oregon. He earned his B.S., Master's and Ph.D. from the University of Oregon, and a certificate in Physical Therapy from New York University. Jim taught school for over 40 years, primarily teaching kinesiology and exercise physiology and coaching track and cross country at universities in California.

# MORRIS Crisci

Morris is a native of San Diego. He grew up in Little Italy. His formal education includes attendance at San Diego State University. He earned his Bachelor's Degree in Mathematics and Music and a Graduate Degree in Education. His unusual career path includes public school teaching, professional opera singing, and construction.

# RITA Early

Rita is a native of Oakland, CA, a U.S. Navy Veteran and a UCLA Bruin. She currently resides in San Diego, California with her hubby, Chris, their little girl, Ladybug, and two mischievous mutts, Kallie and Lilly.

DONNA Ferguson
Donna discovered her love of the written word while still a teenager, mentored by her seventh grade English teacher Helen Tucker, of Miami. She guided, and applauded, but most importantly inoculated me with pride, and belief in my abilities. We communicate often, blessed by our friendship of more than 52 years.

HARRY Field
Author of two novels, *Down by Two* and *Kickin' It*, Mr. Field subscribes to the Elmore Leonard theory of writing: "Try to leave out the parts that readers want to skip." He believes brevity is not only the soul of wit but the heart of poetry. Forty years in San Diego, Harry and his fiercest critic, wife Pat, live in a home on a canyon in South Park.

NANCY Foley
Nancy earned her bachelor's degree from The University of Dayton. Her family moved to San Diego in 1982. After raising four children, Nancy enrolled in creative writing classes at SDSU. Her prose and poetry appear in two anthologies: *For the Love of Writing* and *A Volume of Voices*. Seven grandchildren provide ample material for stories and poems.

PAUL Ford
Paul was born and raised in Los Angeles and moved to San Diego in 1996. As an ex-marine, police officer and past owner of a private investigation firm, he draws on life's experiences for his writing. In retirement, he has been able to pursue this creative outlet.

BIL Fuhrer
Bil grew up in Pennsylvania, graduated from Penn State in Electrical Engineering and moved to California to thaw out. He married his college sweetheart and has two daughters and two grandkids. He's retired, traveling and writing.

MICHELE Garb
Michele graduated from a well-known public university with a degree in computer science. She found work as a software engineer with a leading technology integrator. After 30 years working in the industry, Michele retired and is pursuing her childhood dream of becoming a writer of something other than technical documents.

ELAINE M. Fuller-Zachey
Elaine lives in San Diego, California, with her husband. She has taught English as a Second Language in the San Diego Community College District, Continuing Education, for over 30 years. She is a minister at the Teaching of the Inner Christ where she speaks, leads, writes and teaches.

LLOYD Hill
Lloyd, aka OB Laureate Lloyd and Ocean Beach poet. Longtime coffeehouse bard. Published City Beat 2013, Best of Beach, Christian Science Monitor, Southwestern Literary Journal, A Volume of Voices, Musings winner, Winston's feature. Cartooning as a kid led to fiction and poetry. SDSU, SDCC, SWC; three degrees, 300 units. Leads poet's workshop, Lazy Hummingbird.

# GEORGANNA Holmes

Georganna has self-published several chapbooks of poetry. She is retired from the San Diego Public Library system, and enjoys books so much she now works there as a volunteer.

# MARION Kahn

Marion grew up in New York and lived in seven states before moving to San Diego in 1967 for the sun and sea and a professorship at SDSU. Now retired and free of academia, she enjoys world travel, writing, theatre volunteering and visits with her son and grandsons.

# AVERY Kerr

Avery co-founded Santa Fe Secondary, a unique, private school where she taught English, Latin, and Language Arts to students in grades 7-12. In addition to reading and writing, her passions include swimming, figure skating, and Shakespeare. She currently resides in San Diego.

# REBECCA Johnson

Rebecca grew up in New York, lived with her family in London during her high school years and traveled in Europe. She resides now in San Diego, CA. She studied English and creative writing at college. She likes to write short stories and poetry and has contributed writings in two previous Writer's Workshop anthologies.

DAVID S. Larson
Began writing seriously in 2013, as well as editing and publishing. Author of *WEST: Journey Across the Plains* and *MAYDAY! A Collection of Stories*. Feature screenwriter of *A Silken Thread* (in pre-production) and *Savage Reprisal*. Author of *The Last Jewish Gangster* (producer attached to create multi-part TV program). Signed for representation in 2014 with agency out of CT.

CHERI LaLone
Living a big life is a key element in creating a gifted writer. Cheri has a wealth of events from a colorful past; now in her senior years, they're easy to draw from. Writing in first person draws her readers into a web of intrigue to light a fire and challenge their thinking.

ALASTAIR McAulay
lastair is a graduate of Cambridge University UK and holds a PhD from Carnegie Mellon University. He recently retired from Lehigh University and is currently living in San Diego where he enjoys writing and exploring San Diego with his wife, Carol-Julia.

ROBERT (Bob) McLoughlin
obert was born in Watertown, New York and was a Physics major, graduating from Syracuse University in 1941. He was also the New England States figure skating champion in 1944. CEO of six California corporations from 1957 through 1995. Married teacher, Rhuebelle Bramham, in 1948. He has two sons, five grandchildren, two great grandchildren. Wife, Rhuebelle, died September 2012, after sixty-four years of marriage.

SUSIE Parker
Susie was born to a Navy family. They lived in Arlington, VA; Pensacola, FL; Lake Mary, FL; Falls Church, VA; and, Virginia Beach, VA. When her father retired, the family moved to Tustin, CA. She attended various colleges. She taught in Florida. Susie is now retired. The Writers' Workshop has enriched her life.

KATHERINE A. Porter
While working on two novels, one historical the other whimsical, Katherine enjoys creating mosaic art for her home. In the last two years she earned a Certificate in Copyediting through the UCSD Extension and completed developmental edits of seven book-length manuscripts. Her husband, daughter, grandson, puppy, and poetry are her passions.

FRANK Primiano
Frank has been an engineer, professor, forensic investigator, entrepreneur, salesman, and author. He has published in scientific journals and in engineering and medical textbooks, and was a finalist in the 2008 San Diego Book Awards unpublished novel competition. A Cleveland native, Frank also lived in Philadelphia before moving with his wife, Elaine, to San Diego.

JIRAPORN (Nui) Rehfuss
Nui grew up in Thailand, and earned a BA degree in World History and Sociology from Ramkhumhang University. She moved to the USA, studied English, became a certified Pharmacy Technician, and worked for many years in the field. She enjoys yoga, walking, and world travel – last 19 months: 12 countries on four continents.

LINDSAY Elise Reph

Lindsay is finishing a story about her recovery from a car accident that nearly took her life. She lives in San Diego as a writer, wife, and auntie, delighting in each day's blessings. Chapters from her recovery story were published in the 2010 and 2011 anthologies. Selections herein are from her blog: www.intentionanddelight.com

ROBERT Ross

Robert began his writing career in the mid 1970's by publishing his first article. He's been writing ever since. When not writing, he enjoys playing the classical guitar, skiing, swimming, cycling, and traveling.

DAVE Schmidt

Dave lives in Mission Hills. He grew up in the Midwest and received an M.S. degree in Computer Science from the University of Nebraska in 1985. He completed his computer specialist career in Civil Service at a San Diego DoD lab. His current personal goals include writing poetry related to self-help and personal development.

LINDA Smith

Linda has been writing poetry and short stories since 2010. In February 2011, she joined Writers' Workshop. She is currently working on a memoir and has been living in San Diego, California, her adopted hometown, since 1981. She loves to spend time with family, friends, dogs, and walking on the beach, listening to the ocean.

JEANE Taddonio
Jeane, a longtime member of the SDCC Writers' Workshop,
holds a nursing degree from SDSU. Her poetry and stories
seek to inspire the idea that no thing is ordinary. A children's
story awaits publication. Several poems have been published
in on-line journals and in three class anthologies. Blog site:
jeanetaddonio.wordpress.com.

ERIKA Toraya
A Phoenix native, Erika loves San Diego and the great
outdoors. She enjoys and is inspired by her fellow colleagues
in her Writers' Workshops, acting classes, and Cursillo and
church community. She has been acting in theatre and film
this past year and is grateful to be pursuing her lifelong dream.

JOE Torricelli
Joe was born in 1925 and educated in New York City.
Drafted into World War II, he attended trade school under the
G.I. Bill. Moved to San Diego in 1954, and attended SDSC,
and grad school. He worked as a counselor in private practice.
Retired in 1985 he began writing poetry and novels.

WALLACE Daniel Watson II
Wallace comes from a long line of storytellers. He is the
first to take the craft to paper. Wallace's roots come from an
interesting mix of Native American and Mormon stock,
making him a guide of the most unusual kind! Look for his
first full-length, autobiographical novel to be published soon.

JEFF Curtiss Welch
Born at Sharp Hospital and raised in Lemon Grove, Jeff has resided within San Diego County his entire life; his California upbringing tempered by the world view of his Great Plains-bred parents. Prefers the path less traveled. Favorite authors include Ray Bradbury, John Steinbeck and Douglas Coupland. "Forward – forward!"

Made in the USA
San Bernardino, CA
22 March 2020